The Maintena...

A play

Richard Harris

Samuel French – London
New York – Sydney – Toronto – Hollywood

Adrian Bowd

THE MAINTENANCE MAN

First produced at the Thorndike Theatre, Leatherhead.
Subsequently presented by Bill Kenwright in association
with the Thorndike Theatre at the Comedy Theatre,
London on 1st September, 1986, with the following cast
of characters:

Bob   John Alderton
Christine   Gwen Taylor
Diana   Susan Penhaligon

Directed by Roger Clissold
Designed by Tim Bickerton

The action takes place in the living-room of Christine's
house in North London and the living-room of Diana's
house in West London

Time—the present

ACT I*

The action takes place in the living-room of Christine's house in North London, and the living-room of Diana's house in West London. Both these rooms are represented by the same set

There are two doors. One left, one right. The doors open inwards and are hinged upstage so that a section of the hall outside may be seen. Upstage of each door is a recess in which is a window with plain curtains. These recesses may be used to conceal various items—clothing etc.—for use in scenes as necessary

Beneath the window R is a table holding a radio, vase of flowers etc. There are six non-matching dining chairs distributed throughout the room. There is a sofa and non-matching easy chair. Before the sofa, a coffee table holding a cordless telephone and a box which contains such items as screwdriver, box of matches etc. A low occasional table usually stands next to the sofa: when we first see it, it is being used as a workbench. Downstage, to each side, is a small occasional table with side light. Lights and tables should be of different design. L is an ironing board with iron and half ironed tablecloth. Near it, a small pile of completed ironing. From the ceiling, rear, a pendant light. General evidence of children in the house

There are two sets of wooden shelf units, each about two metres high. The one, R, is complete, varnished, full of books, odds and ends, and is set against the back wall. The one, L, is incomplete, in plain wood, and standing away from the back wall

Before the CURTAIN rises, we hear three commanding knocks with a hammer. Then, quietly at first, the sound of Bob singing and sawing. He is singing "Gonna Build A Mountain". The sounds get louder ... the singing more exuberant, free-form. Then these sounds suddenly stop as the CURTAIN rises

Bob is standing, his back to us, admiring the shelf unit he is building. He's nearly forty. Wears a T-shirt. Having a rest from his labours and smoking a cigarette

A length of wood lies across the occasional table which has been moved out, C. There is a newspaper beneath to catch sawdust. A toolbag and various tools are untidily scattered. They include a battery-driven, cordless drill

Rest over, he stubs the cigarette into an ashtray, takes up a metal tape-measure and, still humming under his breath, moves to measure the width of the unit

Bob Thirty-two and seven-eighths ... (*He repeats this measurement under*

---

*N.B. Paragraph 3 on page ii of this Acting edition regarding photocopying and video-recording should be carefully read.

his breath as he marks up the length of wood on the table with pencil and carpenter's square. All done with the air of someone who knows what he is doing. He is about to saw the wood, when on second thoughts, he goes back and re-measures the width of the unit. Satisfied, he begins to saw)

As he does, Christine enters. She will always enter and exit at the door, L. She is attractive but not pretty. A couple of years older than he is. Manchester accent all but gone after years in the south. She wears grannie glasses for reading

For a moment she stands in the doorway, watching him. He becomes aware of her and offers something of a smile. He gets nothing in return. He resumes sawing

Chris It's half-past six.
Bob Nearly finished.
Chris I've got people coming.
Bob Yes, all right, you said.

She moves in and takes up a small pile of ironing from near the ironing board

Chris I've got things to do—I don't want to be running around clearing up this lot.
Bob Five minutes and I'm done.
Chris It was five minutes yesterday.

She goes out with the ironing. It has been short jabs and evasive action— more the feeling of ritual than of actual combat

He finishes sawing and is sandpapering the wood as:

Christine enters

Bob Do you know how much it would cost to get a bloke to do this? Have you any idea what they charge nowadays?
Chris No and I'm not interested. (*She irons the tablecloth*)
Bob I'll tell you what they'd charge . . .
Chris A fortune.
Bob That's right, a fortune. If you can get hold of one. (*He reverses the shelf and sands the other end*) And even if you could, you'd get a lousy job because they don't care. Four-inch clout nails and a lump of soggy deal. Sixty quid, madam, thank you very much.
Chris Sir.
Bob Eh?
Chris Sixty quid—sir. I wouldn't pay—you would.
Bob No-one's asking you to pay.
Chris Your house.

He sighs dramatically. It's clearly a well-worn pattern

Bob I don't *live* here any more.
Chris All right—your mortgage.

She "smiles". He looks at her, then decides to change tack and indicates the unit with:

Bob Anyway—coming along though, eh?

Chris Be all right when it's finished.

Bob That's what I like—enthusiasm.

Chris What d'you want—a round of applause?

Bob No, I do not want a round of applause—what I would like is a bit of enthusiasm.

Chris I thought you got all the enthusiasm you needed from *her.*

Bob Yeah, yeah, all right, Chris . . .

Chris I expect she gives it to you an' all. She will do. Until she gets fed up with having to give you a standing ovation every time you do something wonderful like getting your bowels moving.

Bob (*taking the shelf to the unit*) You never miss, do you? You never miss the chance of having a go.

Chris You come here, you know what to expect.

Bob Yeah, yeah, yeah. (*He makes to offer the shelf up to the unit, but*) I do not have trouble with my bowels, I never have.

Chris (*derisively*) Huh!

Again he makes to offer up the shelf, but:

Anyway. I didn't ask you to build the bloody thing.

Bob No. No, you didn't ask.

Chris You offered.

Bob That's right. You happened to mention you'd like some more shelves and I offered to build them.

Chris Get on with it then.

Again he is about to offer up the shelf, but:

Bob Whatever I do in this place, I do for you and the kids.

Chris When you're not too busy doing it for her.

Bob Doing what for her?

Chris Whatever it is that makes you so happy.

Bob Happi-er.

Chris (*the sudden dramatic gesture with:*) "Let me have my freedom!"

Bob (*wearily*) I didn't say that.

Chris Oh come off it. (*Again, the drama*) "Let me go before I suffocate!"

Bob You really believe that, don't you? You really believe I said that.

Chris I wrote it all down.

Bob What for?

Chris On the advice of my solicitor.

Bob You could still have made it up.

Chris Not one word. You know very well . . . you sat there . . . tears running down your face . . .

Bob I was upset.

Chris *You* were upset?

Bob *We* were upset.

Chris (*the drama*) "Forgive me, Christine, forgive me!"

Bob I did not ask you to forgive me. What I might have said was ... understand. Understand me, Christine, understand me.

Chris Forgive.

Bob Understand.

Chris I wrote it all down, cleverclogs. (*She switches off the iron and folds the tablecloth and carries it upstage to put it over the back of a chair, during the following*)

Bob Yeah, yeah, all right, you wrote it down.

Chris Understand? Your own mother can't understand you.

Bob That's right, enjoy yourself, bring her into it. (*Again he is about to offer up the shelf, but:*) You mean you actually wrote it all down in a book or something?

Chris That's right. I kept notes.

Bob Why?

Chris Mental cruelty.

Bob Mental cruelty what?

Chris Mental cruelty evidence. So don't call me a liar.

Again he makes to offer up the shelf, but:

Anyway. That's what you do, isn't it? Write things down—"make notes".

Bob I write to earn a living.

Chris Why d'you think *I* did it?

Bob Smart.

Chris At least I told the truth.

Bob And I don't?

Chris Do you?

Bob You live well enough off it.

Chris You think so, you really think so?

Bob Chris—I came here to build these shelves. Not to have a row.

Chris Get on with it then.

Bob All I'm trying to say is—I do things in this house for you and the kids—I do it because I want to.

Chris And because otherwise you'd have to pay someone else to do it.

Bob Because I'd have to pay someone else and because you wouldn't get a good job done anyway.

Chris All right. I accept that.

Bob Thank you. That's all I ask.

Chris I accept it and I'm waiting to clear this room up.

Bob I can't win, can I? (*He makes to take up his cigarette*)

Chris No-one's asking you to win, just to get my shelves up and do you mind not flicking your new ash all over my old carpet?

He looks at her. Then offers up the shelf. This time he actually completes the movement and finds that the shelf is about an inch too short

Bob Shit. (*He wiggles the shelf about on its supports*) Shit shit *shit*.

Chris It doesn't fit.

Bob I know it doesn't fit.

Chris It's too short.

Bob How can it be short, I double-checked.

Chris Perhaps you should have used thicker wood.

Bob It'll be all right. Drop of Polyfilla and you won't know the difference.
    (*He lets go of one end to prove his point. It collapses*)

Chris Right. That's it for the day then, is it?

Bob I suppose so.

Chris I can start clearing up then, can I?

Bob Just let me get my tools out of the way, will you?

They collect up the tools, stuffing them into the bag, and tidy the room a little, folding up the newspaper and putting the low table next to the sofa

    I still can't find my chisel.

Chris What chisel?

Bob My half-inch chisel.

Chris The one *I* bought you?

Bob Good chisel, that is.

Chris You're not accusing me, are you?

Bob I'm not accusing anyone.

Chris Perhaps *she's* got it.

Bob What would she want with a half-inch chisel?

Chris I don't know: some of the things I've heard about her.

Bob You've never met her.

Chris No and I don't want to.

Bob Anyway—what d'you mean—"she"?

Chris *Her.*

Bob She's got a name, you know.

Chris Oh yes—she's got a name all right.

Bob Look—I'm living with her. You can't go on ignoring her—for the sake
    of the kids if nothing else.

Chris Can't I?

Bob We've been divorced for six months for Chrissake, you've got to stop
    talking about her like she's——

Chris I don't want to talk about her. I don't want to see her, I don't want to
    speak to her, I don't want to know anything about her. If you want to
    come here . . . if you want to do things for me . . . do it. But don't keep
    ramming her down my throat. I don't want to know . . . I don't want to
    know.

Up to this moment, it has been the ritual of two people who are fond of each other but can't live together. But now, in this sudden outburst, the first real pain. This moment. Now, both subdued:

Bob I'll—let you get on then.

Chris I've got people coming for dinner, that's all.

He nods. Then makes to move the shelf unit back against the wall. She helps him

    When will you finish it?

Bob Er ... I can't come tomorrow—how about Wednesday?

Chris I think I'm doing something Wednesday.

Bob Yeah—well—I'll—you know—give you a ring. Whenever it's convenient.

Chris What about your work?

Bob I've just finished this script for the Beeb. I was gonna take a few days off anyway. Do a few things. You know.

Chris Are you still working on that police series?

Bob Yeah. (*The thought clearly doesn't please him. He takes up the toolbag*) Say hello to the kids for me.

Chris They'll be sorry they missed you.

Bob Whose party is it?

Chris Paul's.

Bob (*nodding*) How's Loulie's tummy?

Chris All right. Just her age.

A moment

You'll give me a ring then.

Bob (*nodding*) Yeah.

This moment. The two of them together, but not together. The Lights change to bright white lighting DS *and Bob addresses the audience*

Every time ... every time, I swear I'm not going to aggravate her ... I swear I'm going to keep my mouth shut. I even rehearse on the way over. Half an hour it takes me to drive here, during which time I've worked out exactly how the scene should be played ... "Hello Christine, how nice to see you" ...

Chris (*moving* DL *and facing the audience*) "Nice to see *you*, Robert—sit down, I'll make you a cup of tea."

Bob "No, no—you sit down, I'll do it."

Chris But as soon as he walks through that door——

Bob —out go her nostrils——

Chris —up goes his top lip——

Bob ⎫
Chris ⎭ (*together*) and we're at it.

Chris Only why he should think it will be any different ...

Bob Christ—when we were married ...

Chris Not always. Not always.

A slight moment

Bob No. (*He puts down the toolbag and calls*) Anybody home?

Chris Is that you?

Bob No, it's your fancy man.

Chris Not with my luck it isn't—which reminds me—your mother phoned.

Bob And you said I'd fetch her over for the weekend.

Chris *Well*—she's on her own and everything.

Bob Loulie asleep?

Chris Hours ago—where've you been, anyway?

Bob I popped in to see Doctor Kirtley about my back.
Chris I hope you didn't tell him you did it playing Scrabble.
Bob We had quite a pleasant chat, actually.
Chris What about?
Bob This and that.
Chris All he ever says to me is "get your clothes off".
Bob We're all the same—give us a kiss.

This moment

   I love you.
Chris Just as well. I'm pregnant again.

They smile at the memory. Then, back to the present again

Bob The thing is, you see . . .
Chris Stand by for a funny.
Bob I'm always right and she just can't see it.
Chris Laugh? I thought I'd never start.
Bob (*pointing*) Not bad those shelves though, eh?
Chris They don't fit—tell him—they don't fit!
Bob Drop of Polyfilla and you won't know the difference. (*But*) I should
   stay away. Bloody hell, commonsense.
Chris Why doesn't he?
Bob I don't know. I don't know. It wasn't always like this.
Chris For all the shouting and yelling . . .
Bob For all the——
Chris —frustration.
Bob At least I knew where I was supposed to be.
Chris Supposed.
Bob I was here.
Chris And he didn't want to be.

   Chris exits

Bob And I didn't want to be.
Diana (*calling off*) Anybody home?
Bob Now I'm here and . . . and what? (*He slumps into the easy chair, putting
   down the toolbag as:*)

The Lights change—back to evening lighting as before

   Diana enters. She will always enter and exit at the door, R

*She's in her late thirties. Trained as a dancer, she still moves lightly but there's
nothing fey about her. She wears her "business" suit and carries a loaded
M & S bag. She wears large glasses for reading. She tosses a set of keys across
at Bob who automatically catches them*

Diana Bloody car broke down again. (*She deposits the bag*)
Bob What's wrong with it this time?
Diana I've no idea—d'you want some tea?
Bob Yeah—thanks.

She goes out

(*After a pause, calling*) Where is it?
Diana (*off*) Sorry?
Bob (*mumbling*) Doesn't matter . . . doesn't matter.

She comes in

Diana What?
Bob I said—where did you leave it?
Diana Charlotte Street.
Bob You didn't just *leave* it.
Diana On a meter.
Bob You'll get clamped.
Diana I left a note.
Bob I'm surprised you don't get some cards printed.

She "smiles" at him

What excuse did you give this time—not that they're gonna believe you.
Diana (*miming writing*) Sorry: I have broken down.
Bob That should confuse 'em: They won't know whether to contact the AA or The Tavistock Clinic.
Diana Well if they're confused I'm in with a chance, aren't I, you irritable sod.

She goes out

He sees his toolbag and quickly moves it out of sight

Bob How did you get back?
Diana (*calling, off*) On the tube.
Bob Did you get that book?
Diana (*off*) What?
Bob Did you get my book?
Diana (*off*) No.
Bob (*grimacing*) You said you'd get it for me.

She enters with a tray holding two mugs of tea. She gives him one and sits on the sofa

Diana It's out of stock.
Bob Bugger.
Diana I phoned the publishers—they'll have one for me tomorrow afternoon.
Bob Thanks. (*After a slight pause*) You're at the hospital tomorrow.
Diana I'll be finished by three: I'll pick it up then.

A slight moment

Bob And don't forget——
Diana (*joining in*) —to get a receipt.

They sip tea for a moment

And what sort of day have *you* had, Diana?
Bob You've cost me a small fortune, I know that.
Diana When have I ever asked you to pay my parking fines?
Bob The Bank of England couldn't pay your parking fines.
Diana I do work, you know.
Bob Yeah, yeah.
Diana It pays the mortgage.
Bob Only the mortgage.

A moment

Diana Yes. (*She gets up and sorts through the M & S bag—some food, men's socks, girls' panties, a girl's cardigan—during the following*)
Bob So what are we gonna do about the car?
Diana I thought you could run me back there this evening.
Bob I don't know what's wrong with it.
Diana I think it's petrol.
Bob You mean you know it's petrol.
Diana I mean I think I know it's petrol.
Bob How many more times?
Diana It's not me, it's the gauge.
Bob Couldn't you get it to a garage or something?
Diana I was in a hurry to get your book.
Bob I give up.
Diana No you don't, that's your trouble.
Bob What's that supposed to mean?
Diana Don't speak with your teeth clenched.
Bob How can someone so—organized, be so bloody hopeless at times?
Diana (*brightly*) I do it for *you*, darling.
Bob You what?
Diana (*holding up the cardigan*) D'you like this?
Bob That's right—go on—slide out of it.
Diana She did say blue, didn't she?
Bob Don't ask me: where is she anyway?
Diana She went straight to Brownies.
Bob And I've got to collect her, I suppose.
Diana (*mocking, bright*) Would you, darling?

He grimaces, she blows him a cheery kiss

Anyway, it'll be a good excuse.
Bob What will?
Diana Collecting the car. It'll be the first time we've been out together for a week.
Bob I've been trying to finish that lousy script.
Diana How's it coming?
Bob }(*together*) Don't ask.
Diana }
Bob And trying to decorate that bedroom.
Diana You haven't been near it.

Bob I get tired.

Diana We can collect the car and go to the pictures or something.

Bob We haven't got a babysitter.

Diana I'll get a babysitter: all right?

Again the smile that takes the wind out of his sails—but:

Bob Don't get that Julian round here—he drinks all my whisky.

Diana He's worried about his A levels.

Bob I dunno: in my day it was Coca-cola.

Diana I never knew the orphanage could afford such luxuries.

Bob Oh dear—we *are* in a frisky mood, aren't we?

Diana I've been spending money: you know what that does to me.

Bob Anyway. I meant for special occasions. Yeah. Coca-cola and cigarette ash.

Diana I thought you didn't smoke until you were twenty. Or was that another one of your romantic tales of deprivation?

Bob There was this rumour went round that if you put cigarette ash into a girl's drink it made them sexy.

Diana Knickers.

Bob 'Strue.

Diana Knickers. (*After a pause*) Did it?

Bob We never found out: they kept vomiting.

Diana I'm surprised you let a little thing like that put you off.

Bob Funny the way these rumours go round. (*He warms to the subject: never happier than when delving into the past*) We used to have another one about bruised ankles. If you saw a woman with a bruised ankle, it meant she'd just had it off. Not that we knew what having it off meant, mind— but we knew it was dirty. We used to go up the High Street on a Saturday morning and sort of crouch in doorways. With a notebook. Making notes. Age, hair colouring, physical peculiarities, that sort of thing.

Diana You never know when these things come in handy, I suppose.

Bob Me and my friend Alan Longstaffe. He's a chiropodist now, you know.

Diana How old were you?

Bob Mmm?

Diana When you were crawling up and down the High Street.

Bob Oh ... twelve ... thirteen.

Diana Kids nowadays don't know what they're missing, do they?

Bob No violence on the terrace in my day.

Diana Yes, and you always had a clean shirt and a cheery wave for the neighbours.

Bob I suppose you were orf to the country every weekend.

Diana No: Saturday mornings I went to ballet class and bloody hard work it was too.

Bob There y'go, you see ... totally different lifestyle.

Diana You crouching and me stretching. It's a wonder we've got any point of contact at all, isn't it?

This moment

Bob You've got to get rid of that car, Di.
Diana I need it.
Bob It doesn't go.
Diana It always gets me there. It just—doesn't always get me back.
Bob I can't afford to run two cars.
Diana You don't run two cars.
Bob You know what I mean.
Diana I work, I need a car—all right?

A moment. Then she gets up to start folding away the ironing board

Thanks for putting this away.
Bob I've only just sat *down*.
Diana Yes, you look as if you could do with a rest.
Bob I've been *working*.
Diana I thought you could only work in the mornings.
Bob I can only *write* in the mornings. I write in the mornings, sometimes I write at night. The afternoons I like to get away from it, do something different, right? Like what I've been doing this afternoon, decorating that bloody bedroom.
Diana I didn't ask you to decorate the bedroom: I was quite happy to get someone in.
Bob Yeah, yeah.
Diana But *you* said——
Bob All right all right . . . just don't—push me.

She props the ironing board against the wall in the alcove R, *out of sight*

Diana Did anyone phone?
Bob Er . . . no.
Diana I did.
Bob Eh?
Diana I phoned. (*She "smiles"*) No answer.
Bob I went round the pub for half an hour.
Diana At four o'clock.

This moment

Bob All right. I popped over to see the kids.
Diana With your toolbag.
Bob (*sighing, wearily*) If you want to say something, say it.
Diana You were there all yesterday afternoon, now you've been there again today. What is it this time? The drains again? Or are you building her an extension?
Bob If you must know . . . I—promised to put up some shelves.
Diana Then you bloody well *shouldn't* promise.
Bob She wanted me to.
Diana She doesn't want you to: when are you ever going to understand?
Bob So I'm supposed to let them suffer?
Diana Explain to me . . . just explain to me . . . why will they suffer? Why can't someone else put her rotten shelves up?

Bob Well ... for a start ... because it's cheaper. I have to think of these things.

Diana She doesn't want you there.

Bob You don't know her.

Diana I *know*.

Bob She can't—organize anything.

Diana Leave her alone and she might learn.

Bob I just can't turn my back on them.

Diana (*putting the mugs on the tray*) No-one's asking you to turn your back on them.

Bob So what are you asking?

Diana That you grow up. (*She looks at him. Angry, hurt. Then makes to go out with the tray, but:*)

Bob Just a minute.

Diana (*turning; sharply*) What?

Bob The day I stop running up and down fixing your car ... the day I stop carting your kid up and down from school ... the day *you* need a shelf fixing ... that's the day you start complaining.

A moment

Diana (*quietly*) You sod.

Bob Yeah, yeah, that's me. A right sod.

She stands in the doorway R, *holding her look at him*

Chris enters to stand in the other doorway L

None of them will look at, or refer to each other, as the Lights change to bright white lighting DS *and Bob addresses the audience*

The thing about Diana. ... the marvellous thing about Diana ... is that she seemed to understand. I mean ... I said to her ...

Diana The first day he moved in here.

Bob I said ...

Diana "My kids, my family, will always have first call on me."

Bob I mean, Jesus Christ, I feel bad enough about what's happened ... I just can't turn my back on them.

Diana It's not for them. It's for him.

Bob You know what she said—Di? She said ...

Chris (*with an edge*) "That's why I love you so much."

Diana That's why—I love you so much.

Diana exits R

Bob So now I'm here, you see ... I'm here ...

Chris moves into the room, with a newspaper. She sits on the sofa, flicks through the newspaper as:

Flashback. End of March. Eighteen months ago. Christ, was it really eighteen months ago?

The Lights change to evening lighting

He pulls off the T-shirt and puts on a clean shirt as:

Look—are you coming or aren't you?

She ignores him

Why? Just tell me why?

Chris (*reading*) You know perfectly well why.

Bob I don't. I really don't. Explain it to me.

She ignores him, turns a page

All right. I'll go on my own. (*He takes up a deodorant spray and sprays his armpits*)

Chris That's right.

Bob Waddaya mean—that's right?

Chris I mean that's why I'm not going.

Bob That isn't an answer.

Chris I mean I'm not going because you don't want me to go.

Bob What are you talking about?

Chris You don't want to me go—you want to be on your own.

Bob No ...

Chris Oh come off it. You've been picking arguments all week knowing full-well it would end up with me saying "sod you, I don't want to go to the rotten party". Well, I'm saying it: sod you, I don't want to go. So clear off and enjoy yourself.

Bob You really think I'd enjoy myself.

Chris I'm bloody sure *I* would.

Bob All right—you go—I'll babysit.

He sits in the easy chair. Still she ignores him, reading

Chris ... it's not me who's been picking arguments ... it's us. I dunno ... it just seems to be one thing after another.

Chris (*reading*) That's right.

Bob That's all, is it, that's right?

Chris You're right, you're absolutely right. I'm agreeing with you. For the first time this week—including what was supposed to be a happy birthday thank you very much—I'm agreeing with you. Now you can go to your rotten party with a clear conscience.

Bob (*"patiently"*) I'm sorry about your birthday.

Chris So am I.

A moment

Bob Come on.

Chris No.

Bob Why?

Chris (*angrily*) Because I don't want to go to a rotten party!

Bob How do you know it'll be rotten?

Chris If you're there, it's bound to be.

Bob If you're not there, it's bound to be.

Chris (*"sweetly"*) Ahh . . . (*After a slight pause*) Piss off. (*She examines the newspaper*)

Bob Chris . . . I don't want to go on my own. Please.

Chris (*reading*) "An unfortunate setback occurred in the marriage when the husband murdered the wife." That's what I need: a man capable of making a decision.

Bob All right—I will go on my own.

Chris That's what you call making a decision, is it?

Bob (*putting on his jacket*) Go and get the carving knife and I'll make another one.

Chris You go and get the carving knife.

Bob You see? We even argue about the murder weapon.

Chris I don't know why we bother.

Bob Neither do I.

This moment. Each wishing they hadn't said it. He puts on a tie, looking into "the mirror in the fourth wall' as:

You know what'll happen: I'll get drunk.

Chris You always get drunk.

Bob That's because I can't drink.

Chris You don't do so bad.

Bob Goes straight to my head, you know it does.

Chris One drink and you're anybody's, two drinks and you're mine.

Bob More or less.

Chris That's the answer then: you go to the party, have a couple of drinks, I'll stay here, make myself beautiful, then you can stagger back and we can have another go at what is laughingly-known as our sex-life.

Bob It's all my fault, is it Chris?

Chris You're all gong and no dinner. Me? I'm like the piano. I came into this house to be used by someone who openly boasted of his expertise and I haven't been touched for months.

Bob That's the way you see it, is it—"used"?

Chris That's the way I'm beginning to see it, yes.

Bob So we argue all day and then go to bed as though nothing has happened.

Chris You haven't laid a hand on me since Jamie was born and you know it.

Bob That isn't true.

Chris How often then? Go on—say it—and we'll both have a laugh.

A moment

Bob (*gently*) Come on Chris . . . be honest . . . after Jamie was born you didn't want to know.

Chris Given time.

Bob Not just *me*, Chris.

A moment. She sighs

Chris I don't know.

Bob Look—it has been a rotten week——

Chris Week?

Bob It's been a rotten week and I'm sorry. All right—it's my fault, I haven't been feeling up to much lately.

Chris You mean you're ill again.

Bob I'm not always ill.

Chris You always think you are.

Bob (*stiffly*) That is not true.

Chris Look at last week.

Bob I had a fever.

Chris Lying in bed with Vick all over your chest like The Lady of the Camelias.

Bob The Lady of the Camelias did not have Vick all over her chest.

Chris She did in the film, cleverclogs.

Bob I'm very prone to chest trouble.

Chris Not so much prone as prostrate.

A moment

Bob Come on Chris: come with me.

Chris No.

Bob We promised we'd go: just for half an hour.

Chris It's too late to get a babysitter.

Bob We can try.

Chris No.

A moment

Then he makes up the mind he made up long ago

Bob All right then. I'm going. (*Unseen by her, he squirts Gold Spot into his mouth*)

Chris Are you taking a bottle?

Bob I suppose so.

Chris Get me some fags when you're at the off-licence, will you?

Bob I don't want to go on my own.

Chris (*looking at him directly*) Then don't go.

This moment and the Lights change to bright white lighting DS

Bob (*to the audience*) I went. Of course I went.

Chris (*softly*) Please. Please.

Bob Yeah, yeah—I know. And . . . I met Diana.

The Lights change to warm, dim party lighting DS. *A background noise of party music as Chris remains sitting and:*

   Diana enters, holding a glass of white wine

So that Chris is seated between them as:

   (*Brightly*) One dray wait wane. You'd better drink it before it gets cold.

Diana (*sipping her wine, then*) Well then.

Bob Well then.

Diana Bett says you're a writer.
Bob You make it sound even more unlikely than it is.
Diana Mostly television.
Bob Mostly.
Diana She also said you don't like talking about it.
Bob Not much. It depends. I mean I don't mind talking shop with people who actually do it—but outside of that ... that sounds rude. Sorry. I mean I don't mean you. I mean—I like to get away from it, that's all. (*He flinches as though someone has bumped into his back. He dabs himself. Brightly insincere*) Not to worry old chap, old chap—my fault.
Diana Why don't we go into the other room? It's quieter.
Bob Why not?

A moment. Then she goes out

The Lights change to bright white lighting DS. *He addresses the audience*

Look—I can't kid you or anyone—I have not been one hundred per cent faithful—hands up all those husbands here tonight who have? (*He scans the audience, shading his eyes*) Thank you very much.
Chris *You*—not them.
Bob Or is that some sort of justification?
Chris Well is it? Is it?
Bob I dunno. I don't know. But every now and again you meet someone ...
Chris Anyone ...
Bob Someone ... who sets a different sort of bell ringing and you know that's the time to back off, that's the dangerous one, that's when you do back off.
Chris Then why didn't you?
Bob If there's something worth going back *to*.

This moment. Christine exits L

I told her I was married of course. Big deal.

The Lights change to daytime lighting as he looks around the room as though seeing it for the first time

Diana enters R *with two mugs of coffee*

He smiles awkwardly and moves quickly to take one of the mugs

Diana Two sugars.
Bob Thanks.
Diana Sorry about the mug.
Bob Snoopy. My favourite.

She sits on the sofa. He doesn't sit, but instead will move around nervously, as:

I've just been to see my accountant actually. That's why I'm over this way. He's just around the corner. Well—sort of. I mean—you know—near as dammit.
Diana That sounds very grand—your "accountant".

Bob Oh yes—he's one of the joys of being self-employed, is my Mr Patel. The other one's the VAT-man. Actually, I have a lot of trouble with accountants. They keep dying on me. As soon as they've nearly got up to date they're lying in hospital with something terminal. It's got to the state where it's not competence I look for so much as rosy cheeks. (*He sits on the chair, carefully away from her*) You didn't mind me phoning?

Diana No. It was—quite a surprise.

Bob But you didn't mind.

Diana I would have said.

A moment

I suppose, being a writer, you do a lot of—travelling around.

Bob Oh yes, the world is my winkle. No, not really. Depends what I'm working on.

Diana What are you working on now?

Bob What am I working on now ... umm ... I've just started this mini-series for American television—as a vehicle for Dustin Hoffman and Beryl Streep—it's an up-date of the Macbeth story. It's called Death Wore A Kilt.

Diana (*smiling*) I should have remembered not to ask.

This moment

Bob I've been wanting to phone you all week.

Diana I didn't think you would.

Bob You mean you thought I was drunk.

Diana I mean I knew you were married.

A slight moment

Bob You gave me your number.

A slight moment

Diana Yes. And I wanted you to phone. I just wasn't sure—what I would do—if you did.

A moment

Bob How long have you been on your own?

Diana How long have I been divorced? Oh—what—just over a year.

Bob (*nodding*) D'you ever see him?

Diana When he collects Sasha. Our daughter. He's seeing her today actually.

Bob (*concerned*) Oh.

Diana He's picking her up straight from school—she spends the night with him.

Bob (*relieved*) Ah. So there's just the one. Kid.

Diana (*nodding*) And you've got two.

Bob Yes. (*A slight pause*) Two. (*For a moment it looks as if he might start feeling sorry for himself but he changes the subject with:*) I suppose it must be a bit of a strain—you know—running a place on your own.

Diana (*amused*) Looks in a bad way, does it?

Bob No, no—just——

Diana There's always someone in an emergency—if the plumbing goes wrong or anything. Which is pretty much as it was before. He wasn't much of a handyman—it was down to Yellow Pages or to hell with it.

Bob Not like me then. I can't bear paying out money for something I ought to be able to do myself. Anyway . . . I sort of fancy myself as a dab-hand. And it makes a change from sitting on me bum writing fairy stories. I've always had this . . . daft really . . . I've always had this thing about using my hands. Give me a wall to build, a bit of plastering, and I'm at peace with the world. Daft really.

A moment

Diana Where does your wife think you are?

Bob She—never asks.

Diana You mean she trusts you or she doesn't care?

This moment. And then he is on his feet again, with:

Bob Look—I shouldn't have come round here. I shouldn't have telephoned . . . I'm married, the marriage is dodgy to say the least, I shouldn't involve you and I don't know what I'm doing here . . . that is, I do know what I'm doing here and if you want me to clear off then say so because otherwise I'm liable to get involved and then God knows what'll happen.

Diana Which pre-supposes that I've got nothing to do with it.

Bob I mean, what's the good? What's the good of me coming here?

A moment

Diana Have you tried with her? I mean really tried?

Bob Oh lady . . . have we tried. (*After a slight pause*) The truth is . . . probably not. That's me and Chris y'see. (*He holds up two clenched fists*) Boom-boom. Things go wrong . . . whatever you say, whatever you do . . . I dunno. Anyway. It'll sort itself out. One way or another. (*And brightly, and without pausing:*) I suppose you wouldn't like to go to bed for half an hour?

Diana Yes.

Bob Christ, I wish you hadn't said that.

Diana Should I have said no and made it easier?

Bob (*sitting*) I don't know. No. Yes. I don't know. (*He tries to make light of it*) Nothing like a straight answer.

Diana I've thought about you a great deal.

Bob You mean—like that.

Diana Not just like that—no.

Bob Like what then?

Diana Like—what it would be like—just being with you.

A moment. And he nods

Bob Yes.

A moment

What was he like—your old man?

Diana John? Very nice. Very—steady, I suppose you'd say. Likes his glass of beer, goes sailing most weekends. He's a doctor. A good one.

Bob But?

Diana But . . . one day he came home and said he was leaving me. *She's* a doctor. A very—young doctor. They met—would you believe—at a Family Planning Conference.

Bob National Health?

Diana National Health.

Bob They've got a lot to answer for.

Diana Haven't they just?

Bob And you had no idea.

Diana Yes . . . and no. Yes, I had an idea. No, I didn't believe it.

Bob (*thinking of his own situation*) It must have hurt.

Diana Yes.

A moment

Bob What went wrong?

Diana You're married.

Bob Yes?

Diana Then you know what went wrong.

A moment

Bob And you—support yourself.

Diana John gives me so much a week for Sasha. I wouldn't want anything else.

Bob You said you worked at the hospital.

Diana St Bernard's. Yes. I'm a physiotherapist.

Bob Chris doesn't work. She was a secretary. That's how we met. She hasn't worked since we were married.

Diana Does she want to work?

Bob She doesn't need to.

Diana That isn't what I asked.

Bob She's never—said she wanted to.

This moment. Then she stands, with:

Diana More coffee?

Bob Umm . . . yes, thanks . . .

He holds out his mug for her to take. But maintains his hold on the mug. They look at each other. This moment. Then he kisses her tentatively, gently. Looks at her. Then kisses her again, more fully. A moment

I've told you the truth about Chris and me. I'm not playing games.

Diana It doesn't have to happen. We can stop it here and now.

Bob I don't want to stop it. Do you?

Diana No.

Bob Which doesn't mean to say I won't probably end up calling you a whore or something.

Diana Yes. You probably will.

She kisses him gently and goes out with the mugs

For a moment he stands. Shuts his eyes briefly as though trying to shut out what is in his mind. Then:

Bob (*calling*) Diana ... (*He moves towards the bookshelves as:*)

Diana enters

You know when I arrived ... you were on the phone to some bloke ... I couldn't help over-hearing ... that is to say, I listened ... something about some shelves or something.

Diana Yes, I want some more shelves put up—why?

Bob I'll do it for you if you like.

Diana You wouldn't have time.

Bob Yes I would. Anyway. I told you. I enjoy it.

A moment

Diana It seems ...

Bob What?

Diana I don't know. It seems a bit ...

Bob A bit what?

Diana I don't know really. It just seems ... (*suddenly she smiles*) ... I don't know.

Bob Right. Next time I'm over, I'll bring my tools, we'll measure up and get the wood in.

A moment

Diana What about your wife?

Bob She won't know—will she?

A moment

Diana You really mean it, don't you?

Bob Certainly.

The Lights change to bright white lighting DS

(*To the audience*) Certainly.

Christine enters L *with a book and sits on the sofa*

Diana remains in the doorway R *behind her as:*

(*Continuing, to the audience*) When I was a kid we used to go into the park and impress the local talent with a few somersaults and five yards of unarmed combat. A quarter of a century later and I'm doing it with a hammer and chisel.

Chris Why does he have to impress us?

Diana It's what we want.

Chris Is it hell as like.

Diana Think about it.

Chris Oh yes.
Diana ⎱
Chris ⎰ (*together*) Little Women.
Diana You're so *strong*.
Chris Yummy-yum.

Diana exits R

Christine lies full-length on the sofa as Bob continues:

Bob But notice wherein lies the concern. Come to bed with me. Certainly. Let me impress you with a bit of shelf-building. What about your wife? What conclusion do I form? That you can screw a woman but you can't screw anything into her wall because that ... that ... is commitment. (*This moment. Then he turns to look at Christine*)

The Lights change to dim evening lighting. The lamp R *is on. The radio is playing softly. Christine is asleep, mouth open. He looks at her, guiltily looks at his watch, then moves across to take up the book which has slipped from her fingers. A Heyer romance. He looks down at her, not without tenderness. Reaches down and gently pushes back a strand of hair that has fallen across her brow. Remains looking at her for a moment and then begins to gently shake her with:*

Chris ...

She protests in heavy sleep

Come on, love.

Again she protests, but opens her eyes ... sees him, is aware that her mouth has been open and is embarrassed, annoyed, at being caught like it. She sits up, moistening her lips. He moves upstage to switch off the radio and sits in the armchair, loosening his tie as:

Chris What's wrong?
Bob Nothing's wrong—go to bed.

She looks at him, still half-asleep. He sits. She gropes for a cigarette, finds the packet empty, decides not to bother

Chris What's the time?
Bob Er ... quarter to ten.
Chris (*looking at her own watch*) It's ten o'clock.
Bob Yeah, all right, I'm slow.
Chris You said nine o'clock at the latest.
Bob It went on. Kids all right?
Chris Why shouldn't they be?
Bob I'm just asking.
Chris When have they ever not been "all right"?

A moment. He can't resist, lying

Bob I did phone—what, about half-eight.

Chris I was bathing the kids.

Bob (*as though remembering*) Oh yeah.

Chris You couldn't have let it ring for long.

Bob I was at a meeting.

Chris Until ten o'clock.

Bob We had a drink, I'm very sorry. (*A slight moment. Then, winging it, guiltily*) Anyway . . . they like the script thank God. Just a couple've tidges here and there, cut down on the filming, get rid of a couple of characters. The usual.

Nothing from her

Well show *some* interest.

Chris I was asleep.

Bob You just don't show any interest whatsoever.

Chris Don't bloody well come that one.

Bob Well do you?

Chris *You* want to talk about your work all of a sudden, we have to talk about it . . . *you* want to shut yourself in your room all day and then come down here with a face like a bucket, we have to put up with it . . . on your terms, everything on *your* terms.

Bob What d'you mean—"we"?

Chris What d'you think I mean?

Bob I'm asking you.

Chris The kids, you bloody idiot.

Bob What about the kids?

Chris You think they don't know something's going on?

A moment

Bob What d'you mean—going on?

Chris Us. Mummy and Daddy. You and me. Hitler and Little Dorritt.

A moment. He fingers his eyes wearily

Des came round.

Bob Oh yeah—what did *he* want?

Chris He wanted to borrow your drill.

Bob (*guiltily, quickly*) What drill?

Chris How many drills have you got?

Bob You mean my electric drill?

Chris I suppose that's what he meant: anyway, he looked in your shed and he couldn't find it.

Bob It's not there.

Chris He says you've been having a clear-out by the look of it.

Bob What's he talking about?

Chris He couldn't find any of your tools.

Bob He's got a bloody cheek looking.

Chris What are you getting so mithered about?

Bob I don't like people poking about in my shed. Workshop. As a matter of fact . . . I've got a lot of stuff in the car. I was going to fix those cupboards for my mother.

Chris She phoned.

Bob Who?

Chris Your mother.

Bob What for?

Chris To tell you about her legs. You weren't here, so she told *me*.

Bob (*wearily*) Oh yeah.

Chris You said you'd phone her.

Bob Yes, I will, I will.

Chris To say when you'll be round to fix the cupboards.

Bob I do work, y'know.

Chris You shouldn't have offered.

Bob I'm her son.

Chris She's beginning to wonder.

Bob I can't keep running round there.

Chris She said you promised to go yesterday.

Bob I . . . got held up.

Chris You told me you played golf.

Bob That's right—I fancied a game of golf—OK?

A moment

Chris Why don't you pay someone to do it for her? You can afford it.

Bob I'll do it.

Chris Then stop complaining.

A moment

Bob You're not going to bed then.

Chris When I'm ready.

Bob (*a decision*) Right: I'm going up. (*He makes to go out, but:*)

Chris He's worried about you.

Bob Who is?

Chris Des, who d'you think?

Bob What's he been saying?

Chris You'd better ask him.

Bob I'm asking you.

Chris He's worried about *us*.

Bob You mean you've talked to him.

Chris No: I assumed you had.

Bob No.

Chris Well . . . you know what he's like.

Bob I suppose it's obvious.

Chris What?

Bob Us. You and me. Next time, tell him to mind his own business. Give me a shout in the morning, will you—I'll take the kids to school. (*He makes to go out, but:*)

Chris Bob.

Bob What now?

Chris Tell me about the meeting.

Bob You're interested, are you?

Chris Forget it.

Bob One minute you're——

Chris Forget it.

Bob I come home with every intention of making an effort . . . I come home . . . and the first thing I see is you lying there with your mouth open like some flaming great porpoise.

Chris I'm *tired*.

Bob It's so . . .

Chris So what?

Bob It doesn't matter.

Chris So *what*?

Bob So bloody ugly.

A moment

Chris Anything else?

A moment

Bob I'm sorry.

Chris You can sleep where you like—you're not coming into *my* bed.

Bob (*moving to her*) Chris . . .

And he puts his arms on her shoulders . . . and suddenly she is whirling round . . . trying to strike at him . . . and he is trying to grab her wrists . . . and they struggle violently, falling back on to the sofa

We've got to stop all this!

Chris You sod. (*And she pulls herself free, her chest heaving*) I am ugly. I look ugly and I feel ugly and I hate you for it. (*She moves to the door, but turns to look at him, suddenly controlled*) Have you got another woman?

Bob No.

Chris Then you'd better find one.

She goes out

For a moment he stands. Then as the Lights change to bright lighting, he quickly pulls off his jacket and shirt and pulls on the T-shirt. He sets up the two dining chairs downstage, takes out his toolbag, saw, cordless drill, sets a plank of wood across the chairs and begins to saw. All this as:

Bob (*to the audience*) Every Sunday, my father would disappear down into his shed whereupon he would slip into something dirty and build shelves. Shelves with no particular purpose other than to support the materials from which he would fashion further shelving. I was never allowed into that shed . . . on my mother's part because it was too would you believe dirty-down-dere . . . and my father's part because I got in the way of what, had he lived longer, must surely have started a new paragraph in the *Guinness Book of Records*. (*By now he is about to saw, but:*) Two hours before he went into hospital to give his stomach to a surgeon, he was out doing the weekend shopping and my mother was ironing his pyjamas. (*He begins to saw*)

Diana enters to stand in the doorway, R, *looking at him*

The Lights change to daytime lighting, Bob becomes aware of Diana

Ow d'you do.

Diana Can I get you anything?

Bob (*sawing*) Cuppa coffee.

Diana Don't you want anything to eat?

He shakes his head. She moves into the room. He indicates the shelving

Bob Not bad, eh?

Diana I think it's marvellous.

Bob Not bad though, eh?

Diana It is, it's marvellous.

Bob I mean, when you think what it would've cost.

Diana I know.

Bob And you wouldn't get a decent job done. They don't care, you see.

He resumes sawing. She moves behind him, kisses his back. He will continue sawing throughout

Diana Are you sure you don't want anything?

Bob Positive.

Diana Nothing at all?

Bob Nothing at all.

Diana You haven't stopped.

Bob I know what I'm like, if I don't keep at it, I'll never finish.

She watches him for a moment. Then puts her arm around him from behind, putting her head against his back. He will try to continue sawing as:

Diana I wish you would.

Bob What?

Diana Stop.

Bob I wish you would.

Diana What?

Bob Stop it.

Diana Don't you like it?

Bob Yes, but . . .

Diana You mean there's a time and a place.

Bob Sort of.

Diana I thought this was the time and the place.

Bob I thought you wanted these shelves put up.

Diana I didn't think you meant non-stop. (*She moves away, sees his cordless drill and takes it up. She poses with it, like a magician's assistant*) We have these cosy little afternoons, you see. Just him, me and his Black and Decker.

Bob Oh, there it is—thanks.

*He takes the drill from her and drills four holes into the shelf he has just sawn
as Diana sits on the coffee table, hands on chin, regarding him*

Diana I had a dream about you last night.
Bob What sort of dream?
Diana That sort of dream.
Bob Dirty cow.
Diana Mmm . . . it was lovely.
Bob Tell us then.
Diana You won't laugh?
Bob How many more times?
Diana You know last week . . . when you were trying to dig that tree out of
    the garden . . . I stood watching you . . . out of the bedroom window . . .
    the muscles in your back as you were pulling it . . .
Bob Bloody roots went down for ever.
Diana I really wanted you. There. In the garden. All sweaty. And in my
    dream . . . I had you.
Bob Was I any good?
Diana Average.
Bob That's right—spoil it.
Diana I love your back.
Bob It flamin' aches, I know that.
Diana I just love . . . looking at it.
Bob You're looking at peoples' backs all day long.
Diana Not the same, shut up.
Bob You mean it's the T-shirt you fancy.
Diana You see, you're laughing at me.

*He smiles, moves to her. She turns her head as though embarrassed. He gently
turns her head and kisses her*

Bob You are. You're daft.
Diana Why am I?
Bob Love looking at me.
Diana Well I do.
Bob What am I supposed to say to that?
Diana You're not supposed to say anything.

A moment

Bob I just don't know how to cope when you talk like that. You just—say
    things.

A moment

Diana Doesn't Chris say anything nice to you?
Bob (*reprimanding*) Oi.

A moment

Diana Sorry.

A moment

Bob No. (*After a slight pause*) That's not true. She used to, I suppose. But then I don't exactly shower her with compliments nowadays, do I?
Diana I don't know.
Bob You do know.

A moment. And he gets on with his work

Diana Are you going to that party with her this weekend?

A slight moment

Bob Yes.

A slight moment

Diana I wish you weren't.
Bob Don't pressurize me, Di.
Diana I'm not.
Bob You are.

A moment

Diana Yes. I am. I don't want to, but I am.

A moment

Bob I'm gonna tell her, Di.

Nothing from her

You think I'm wrong.
Diana You mean to tell her about me.
Bob I can't lie to her. Not any more.
Diana Perhaps she'd prefer you to lie.
Bob It isn't just because of you. If it wasn't like it is, there wouldn't be a you. There's nothing left.
Diana The children.
Bob The kids—yeah. But that's all. It's just—hopeless.

A moment

Diana Are you saying you're going to leave her?

A moment

Bob I don't know. Christ, I don't know.

A moment

Diana You did say you wanted some coffee.
Bob (*nodding*) Yeah. Thanks.

She moves to the door, but:

Diana It is because of me. If you tell her, don't expect her to think anything else. And don't for God's sake expect her to understand.

She goes out

*He stands for a moment. Then takes the shelf to the unit, is about to offer it up
... then turns and looks at the audience as if to say "You don't think this is
going to fit, do you?" This moment. Then with a quick movement, he puts the
shelf into place, banging it down on its supports. It fits perfectly. The Lights
change to bright lighting DS. Bob turns the two chairs so that they are close
together downstage, puts his tools into the bag and puts on a raincoat*

> *During this, Chris enters to stand by the door. She wears a topcoat, clutches
> two full shopping bags—full of Christmas presents for the family*

And throughout all this, Bob addresses the audience

Bob I know this fellah—married man, coupla kids, can't keep his eyes or his
hands off other women. Known for it. One night he comes home after a
particularly frenzied session, scratches all over him. So he strangles the
cat, wakes up his wife, and tells her it attacked him. I am bewildered: how
do you get away with it? Only one thing you've got to remember, son, he
says—a woman can stand anything but the truth. You've got to leave 'em
a way out. Telling a woman the truth is nothing short of self-indulgence.

Chris moves to sit on one of the chairs, looking straight ahead, with:

Chris He indulged himself on the Piccadilly Line between Manor House
and Cockfosters.

*The Lights change, dimming, so that only the area around the chairs is lit. At
the same time, the low sound of an underground train*

> We'd been Christmas shopping.
Bob She'd got a seat—I had to stand for most of the way back.
Chris He stood there—looking at me.
Bob She kept glancing up at me—giving me a little smile——

Which she does now

—but as though to reassure herself, not me.
Chris I was afraid.
Bob Jesus God, what am I doing to her?

*She reacts as though the seat next to her has become vacant, indicates for him
to sit. He does so. They both remain looking straight ahead. This moment and:*

> What would you say ... if I told you ... I've got another woman.

This moment. Both still looking straight ahead

Chris Have you?
Bob I've got to tell you, Chris: it's gone too far.
Chris Are you frightened I'll hit you or something? Is that it—protecting
yourself—thinking I won't do it on a train full of people?
Bob I dunno. Yeah, I suppose it is, in a way.
Chris You coward. (*She gets up*)

*The Lights change to dim lighting. She moves directly to put the bags on to the
sofa and take up her cigarettes and matches from the coffee table. Her hands*

are shaking so much that she spills matches. Bob moves the two chairs and turns on the lamp L and the main light. He moves to her, holding out his lighter. She ignores it, lights her cigarette with a match

How long has it been going on?

Bob (*lying*) Coupla months. Something like that.

Chris What are you going to do about it?

Bob I don't know.

Chris Then you'd better bloody well find out.

Bob It's not just her though, is it Chris?

Chris You're married.

Bob We're not happy—either of us—I'm not happy, you're not happy . . .

Chris I wouldn't open my legs for the first man who came sniffing.

Bob It isn't like that.

Chris Oh no, she's bloody wonderful.

Bob It isn't a question of——

Chris Does she know you're married?

Bob Yes.

Chris But she isn't like that.

Bob No.

Chris You stupid little sod.

This moment

What have you told her?

Bob About what?

Chris About *us*.

Bob Chris, what's the point in——

Chris I want to know—what have you told her?

Bob The truth.

Chris You know all about the truth, do you?

Bob All right—what I feel—what I think's happened to us.

Chris And she understands, does she?

Bob If you like.

Chris If I like.

Bob For God's sake, what can I *say*?

Chris But you've discussed it with her.

Bob You *asked* me.

Chris What have you told her about me?

Bob Nothing.

Chris Of course you have.

Bob Not what you think.

Chris I suppose you told her it's all my fault.

Bob I've told her the truth—that we just don't get on any more.

Chris No doubt she was very pleased.

Bob Of course she wasn't pleased.

A moment

Chris You think I didn't know there was someone else?

Bob I suppose you must have done.
Chris Of course I bloody knew.
Bob Then why didn't you say something?
Chris Because it wasn't worth it.

This moment. She doesn't believe it and neither does he. But no retractions

Bob That just about says it all, doesn't it?

A moment

Chris What's she like?
Bob You don't want to know.
Chris I'm asking you.

A moment

Bob She's—I dunno—she's—(*a slight pause*)—Chris.
Chris I want to *know*.
Bob She's divorced. Got a kid. A little girl. She—works in a hospital. A
     physiotherapist.
Chris You should be well-suited then.

A moment

   Where did you meet her?
Bob At Bett's party.
Chris You said you'd only known her two months.
Bob Yes.
Chris That was in March—why lie?
Bob I don't *know*, Chris.
Chris What difference d'you think it would make?
Bob I don't know, I honestly don't know.
Chris Honestly don't know.
Bob *No.*

A moment

Chris Why don't you say it—you don't love *me*.
Bob Chris.
Chris Do you?
Bob We don't even like each other—that's what's so bloody awful.

A moment

Chris I see.
Bob Well do we?

A moment

   I didn't mean that.
Chris *You're* unhappy—what the hell do *I* get out of it?
Bob That's exactly what I'm *saying*.
Chris I could understand you going with some silly little eighteen year old—
     but a divorcee with a kid—you must be out of your mind.

Bob It isn't her!

Chris Of course it's bloody her!

Bob Listen to us! We talk round and round in circles—it's hopeless, bloody hopeless . . .

Chris The truth? When have *you* ever faced up to the truth about *anything*?

Bob You see?

Chris She was available—you weren't. (*Two of the shelves have been resting against the* UL *wall. With a sudden, angry gesture she hurls them to the floor*) You're a writer, aren't you—well sod off and write a few cheques for your tart and don't bother to write anything to us because we're not interested—not me, not the kids, no one. You've forgotten all about them, haven't you? The kids you're supposed to love so much.

Bob You know what I think about my kids.

Chris It bloody looks like it. They're frightened to show their faces, the mood you've been in the past couple've weeks.

Bob That's what I'm trying to say, Chris—that's what happens.

Chris Then you should have bloody thought about it last March, shouldn't you, you selfish sod.

A moment

Bob Doesn't it mean anything to you, Chris? The fact that I can even think about walking out on my family? Don't you think I haven't worried myself sick about those kids?

Chris You're not thinking of anybody but yourself and you know it.

Bob Not true.

Chris The whole world revolves around you: my God, your mother's got a lot to answer for.

Bob Why do you think I told you, Chris—*why*?

Chris Because you're that bloody stupid.

A moment

Bob I don't want to hurt you, Chris, I swear I don't.

Chris But you'd rather be with her.

A moment

I suppose you think you're in love with her.

A moment

You've known her five minutes and you're in love.

Bob Isn't that what happens? You meet someone, you fall in love—then you get to find out what you've fallen in love with. Wasn't it like that with us.

Chris I see.

This moment. Then he sits in the chair

Bob The best thing I can do is move out.

Chris You mean live with her.

Bob I didn't say that, Chris.

Chris You—live on your own?

Bob Until we get things sorted out—yes.

Chris You can't live on your own—you can't even boil an egg.

Bob I'll have to learn, won't I?

A moment

   We can't go on like this, that's all I know.

A moment. He stupidly attempts a joke

   The trouble is—I've grown even more lovable and you just can't see it.

Chris Oh my God . . . (*She moves across the room*) Save your wrought-irony for your tart: she'll find it funny until she has to live with it: (*By now she is at the door*) If you move out of here, you don't come back.

Bob You mean divorce.

Chris You move out, you don't come back.

Bob You mean you'll divorce me.

Chris Just as soon as you walk through that door.

Bob That's it, Chris—that's us.

Chris That's *you*, mister.

Bob Fight fight fight—all the way.

Chris You've picked the wrong woman if you think you're going to walk all over me.

   And she goes out quickly

He remains sitting in the chair. Then he notices the power drill down by the side of the chair. He takes it up. Looks at it. Then holds it up alongside his head and switches it on. He sits looking straight ahead as . . .

   Chris and Diana enter to stand in the doorways looking at him

At the same time . . . the sound of the drill magnifies . . . then the magnified sound of drilling and hammering . . . then the magnified sound of drilling and hammering and sawing . . . and at the same time the Lights are dimming so that only the area around Bob is lit and——

                    the CURTAIN *falls*

ACT II

The same

Before the CURTAIN *rises, we hear the magnified sounds of sawing, drilling and hammering. Then of drilling and hammering. Then of drilling. Which stops as the* CURTAIN *rises*

The second shelf unit is now finished and set back against the rear wall. A third section has now been put centrally so that the entire rear wall is now covered in dressed shelves. A further shelf unit, about a metre high and unfinished, stands upstage

Bob is sitting in the chair as at the end of Act I. Diana stands in her doorway, holding a shirt which she is folding. Chris stands in her doorway, polishing a child's shoe with a duster

Bob (*to the audience*) My mother runs a very clean house. It is spotless. Her proudest boast is that she could take Royalty into her bathroom. I mention this for the benefit of any member of the Royal Family who happens to be passing through Peckham.

He stands and gives the drill to Chris and the raincoat to Diana who hangs it in the recess, R, *as:*

Just recently, I've had this recurring dream about standing in front of a firing squad while my mother flits around me with a Brillo pad in one hand and a testimonial from the Duke of Edinburgh in the other. (*A slight pause*) I left home, moved into a room on my own.

Diana One room.

Bob The ridiculous to the even more ridiculous.

Chris He said it.

Bob I didn't just walk out ... I mean, not just like that ...

Diana There was all the coming and going.

Bob All the attempts to find some sort of common ground.

Chris But ...

Bob Nothing. (*A moment*) I nearly found myself a flat—couple've rooms, K and B, the complete ensemble.

Chris This woman living on her own in a big house in Highgate.

Diana A friend of a friend of a friend.

Bob I went to see her one Sunday morning. She was with this little Irish chippie who did things for her.

Diana
Chris } (*together*) Oh yes?

Bob She told me how expensive he was and I actually heard myself offering to put in a window-frame.

Diana Luckily young Patrick stepped up the blarney and all was saved.

Chris But he offered, he actually offered.

She goes out

Bob We had a cuppa coffee together and she told me what a swine her husband had been. I must have looked very understanding because she offered me one of her Valiums. I started to tell her about my situation but it became very clear that a problem shared was a problem she didn't want to know about. She said she'd give me a ring, let me know about the flat. That was the last I heard of her. (*He grins ruefully at the thought. Then takes a rag from his pocket and is wiping his hands as:*)

The Lights change to evening lighting—table lamps and main light on

Diana (*calling upstairs from the door*) Go to sleep! (*She moves back into the room, taking up a discarded book, felt-tip pens, a cardigan*) She's being a right little mare.

Bob Not because of me, is it?

Diana No, no—she's just got it on her. You know what they're like sometimes.

A moment. And he gives a little nod, with:

Bob Yeah. (*He digs into a pocket to pull out her car keys which he holds up with:*) All done.

Diana Does it go?

Bob Sort of.

She takes the keys, kissing his cheek

Diana Thanks.

He sits wearily on the sofa, realizes he is sitting on something and pulls out a child's shoe which he holds out to Diana who takes it and searches for the other one

What was it?

Bob The plugs.

Diana I'm never quite sure what the plugs *do*.

Bob In your case—just lurk there, gathering moss. Anyway, they're clean enough now—but I'd get a new set fitted if I were you. Or better still, keep the plugs and throw the car away.

Diana It's not a bad little car—it just needs looking after.

She puts the things she has collected on to the table, UR, then comes to sit next to Bob who puts an arm around her, kissing her brow. She snuggles close, putting an arm across his chest, closes her eyes. Hold this. And:

(*Eyes still closed*) What are you thinking?

Bob I'm thinking . . . how much my back aches.

Diana (*eyes still closed*) Have a bath.

Bob I'll have one when I get back.

A moment

Diana D'you share a bathroom?
Bob Mmm.
Diana Must be awful.
Bob Not so much awful as desperate—especially at ten to eight in the morning. I'm nothing if not regular which is very hard to explain to two young ladies and an Indian you've only seen the back of.

A moment

Diana You know you can't move in with me. It would confuse things, you're supposed to be sorting yourself out. If you're here . . .
Bob (*nodding*) Yeah, yeah. (*It's not the first time she has said it*) I called in at the estate agent's this afternoon. Ah yes, he said, I think we might have something for you—just come on the market—very spacious, very sunny—I think you'll like it.
Diana And?
Bob There was more space and sunshine in the boot of his Porsche. D'you think I've strained it?
Diana What?
Bob My back.
Diana I've no idea.
Bob You don't think I've slipped a disc, do you?
Diana I shouldn't think so for one minute.
Bob Oh.
Diana I suppose you think I should examine you or something.
Bob There was a time you couldn't keep your hands off it. You said my back was lovely.
Diana I still think it's lovely. I expect your GP will say the same.
Bob Thanks.

A moment

Diana D'you know how many vertebrae you've got?
Bob (*considering, then*) Thirty-seven.
Diana D'you know how many vertebrae everyone else has got?
Bob No.
Diana Twenty-four.
Bob Ah yes—but I'm a member of BUPA. (*A moment*) I called in to see him this morning.
Diana Who?
Bob My doctor.
Diana Why? To get your season ticket?
Bob To pick up my prescription. He was a bit quiet so we had a chat. Tell me, doctor, I said, what is the most important thing you have discovered about the human condition? I'll tell you, he said. The most important thing I have discovered about the human condition is that man spends the first half of his life trying to make money and the second half trying to

make water. (*A moment. And he sits up with:*) Oh well, I'd better be going I
suppose.

Diana Will you be over for a meal tomorrow?

Bob Er ... I'm not sure ... I said I'd go over and see the kids.

Diana (*nodding*) Fine.

Bob I've got to see them, Di.

Diana Of course you've got to see them.

Bob I just—I just can't help worrying about them, that's all.

She kisses him lightly

Diana I love you.

Bob Every time I'm there and the phone rings, she answers it as though it's
someone she doesn't want me to know about—and it never is and I have
to sit there looking like I'm trying not to look interested. It's all such a
terrible bloody game.

Diana (*an edge*) You know why she does it.

Bob It turns my stomach over—not for me, for her.

Diana What happens when it's not a game?

Bob Another fellah, you mean?

Diana It's bound to happen.

Bob I hope it happens. But not yet: not Chris.

She has moved away from him

What happened when your old man went?

Diana D'you really want to know?

Bob That bad, is it?

Diana If you really want to know, I savaged every pair of pants within a
fifteen-mile radius and when I'd done that, I freshened up my lipstick and
doubled the mileage.

Bob (*disparagingly*) Oh yeah?

Diana You don't know whether to believe it or not, do you?

Bob You could have done for all I know.

Diana Thank you.

A moment

Bob You didn't, did you?

Diana No I didn't. But I might have done. It was touch and go. The
slightest touch and off I went.

Bob But they came a-knocking.

Diana A divorcee? Didn't you know—we're desperate. I'd change the
subject if I were you, Bob ...

Bob You slept with me. Married man, the lot.

Diana And I've no excuses to offer. Have you?

A moment

Bob Christ. I don't want to go back to that bloody room.

Diana I don't want you to go back.

Bob I hate it.

Diana You can't stand being on your own, can you?
Bob No, I bloody hate it. (*A moment. Then, without looking at her*) Just tonight.
Diana You said you wouldn't ask.

A moment

Bob Please.

A moment. Then she moves to the door with:

Diana I'll run you a bath.

> *She goes out* R

He stands—and to blank out the knowledge of the step he has just taken:

Bob Di ...

> *Diana enters to stand by the door*

You said something about this light bulb. (*He indicates the pendant light*)
Diana Yes, I don't know what it is, it just won't come out.
Bob I'll have a look at it—turn it off, will you?

She switches off the light as he takes a chair and places it under the pendant

Diana Careful of your back.
Bob (*reacting quickly*) Eh?
Diana I was being funny.
Bob Ho-ho. (*He stands on the chair and attempts to get the bulb out*) Stone me. How long has it been like this?
Diana I can't remember. Ages.
Bob Stone me. I don't know how you do it.
Diana Leave it.

> *She goes out* R

Bob I dunno: women.

> *Christine enters* L, *carrying a bulb in a box*

Chris This is the only one I can find.

They will initially be excessively polite towards each other

Bob What size is it?
Chris What d'you mean—what size?
Bob It'll be on the box—hundred watts, hundred and fifty ...
Chris Hundred and fifty.
Bob That'll do. (*He exchanges the new bulb for the old as:*)
Chris I couldn't move it at all.
Bob They get a bit tight sometimes. (*He tries the light and it works*) Anyway—all done.
Chris Thank you.

He puts his head out of the door to call:

Bob Go to sleep!

Chris They don't need you shouting at them.

Bob Chris—the whole point is for me to behave exactly the same as if I was still here . . .

Chris That's right—shouting at them all the time.

Bob I do not shout at them all the time and you know it. I've got to chastize them every now and again, for God's sake.

Chris Why?

Bob Because I'm their father, they expect it.

Chris Pity you didn't think of that when you met your tart.

Bob Chris . . .

Chris I'm not arguing with you—if you want to argue with someone, argue with her. (*And she shouts out of the door*) Go to sleep!

He takes up the electric iron from the table DL *and a small screwdriver and is sitting, looking at the plug*

Bob Wire's come loose.

Chris sits. A moment

Chris Who does your washing?

Bob (*evading*) Sorry?

Chris Who's doing your washing?

Bob (*lying*) Launderette.

Chris You don't know what a launderette is.

Bob I've found out, haven't I?

Chris What about your good shirts?

Bob I send them to the laundry.

A moment

Chris What about meals?

Bob Most of the time I eat out. There's a—café. It's not bad. Little Greek place. Chicken and chips.

Chris You're not depriving yourself then.

Bob No. No, I'm not depriving myself. Would you prefer me to——

Chris I'm just asking—OK?

A moment

The dog's not eating.

Bob I thought she was looking a bit sorry for herself.

Chris Hasn't touched anything for two days.

A moment

Bob *You're* all right, are you?

Chris I've got to be, haven't I?

Bob Yes, all right Chris, I'm just asking.

Chris And I'm telling you, aren't I?

He indicates the iron, puts it on the side table

Bob There y'go. Nothing else is there?

Chris Not unless you want to put the fence up.

Bob It's not down *again*, is it?

Chris This morning.

Bob Yeah—well—I'll have a look at it this weekend.

Chris I'll get someone in.

Bob No, no, I'll do it. (*A moment. He attempts a smile*) Well, I'll—er—say good-night to the kids then. (*He moves to the door, but:*)

Chris I phoned this house you're supposed to be staying in.

Bob When?

Chris You weren't there.

Bob *When?*

Chris Last night.

Bob I told you—I went to the pictures.

Chris She said they hadn't seen you for days.

Bob I've hardly seen a soul since I've been there.

Chris No?

Bob No! Have you got any idea what it's like living in a bloody *room*?

Chris You could have found somewhere better.

Bob In time I will.

Chris It suits the image: poor little hard-done-by Robert.

Bob Is that what you think?

Chris I'm bloody sure of it.

Bob It's all I could *get*.

Chris You're never *there*.

Bob What d'you mean, I'm never there?

Chris You're with *her*.

He almost replies angrily but:

Bob Why did you phone?

Chris That's my business.

Bob Checking up on me?

Chris On you? I wouldn't lower myself.

Bob You were checking up on me.

Chris You left the number, didn't you?

Bob In case something *happened*.

Chris Why don't you sod off?

Bob Just as soon as I've said good-night to the kids——

Chris Tell me the truth!

Bob All right! I'm living with her! Is that what you want to hear? I'm living with her!

They look at each other angrily. Now she's got the truth, she doesn't quite know how to cope

(*Quietly*) I couldn't stand being in that ... bloody room.

A moment. He moves slowly towards the door, but:

Chris I want some more money.

Bob (*wearily*) What d'you mean—more money?

Chris I need more money.

Bob For Chrissake—I pay the housekeeping, I pay every other bill in the place——

Chris When did you last go shopping?

Bob I pay you good money every *week*.

Chris It's not enough.

Bob Well it's all you're bloody getting.

Chris Then your children will starve.

Bob Don't talk rubbish.

Chris They'll go without while you look after your tart and her kid. Go and explain it to them.

Bob She *works*.

Chris If you can call it work.

Bob Look—I'm not arguing with you ...

Chris I really feel sorry for you, d'you know that? It's not only her you're taking on—you've got a kid as well ... that's two wives and three kids you're supporting ... not to mention the rent you pay for your mother ...

Bob Who said anything about marrying her?

Chris I know you: you're pathetic.

Bob (*"patiently"*) I'm not supporting them—she works.

Chris D'you think she's going to carry on working—now she's got a mug like you to support her?

Bob And I'll tell you something else—you might have to work.

Chris Oh no.

Bob Oh yes.

Chris Why? So you can spend it all on your tart?

Bob Christ! It's hopeless. Why can't you be——

Chris What—civilized?

Bob Yes—all right—civilized!

Chris We didn't have a civilized marriage—why the hell should you expect a civilized divorce?

A moment

Bob Look. I've no intention of depriving you or the kids of anything. You know bloody well I'll give you everything I can.

Chris I don't want to talk about it, I'll talk to my solicitor.

Bob But for God's sake, I've got to have some life of my own.

Chris I don't want to talk about it.

A moment

Bob Yeah, yeah, all right—go and see your solicitor.

Chris And I'm afraid you won't be able to have the kids this Saturday.

Bob What d'you mean?

Chris My mother's coming down.

Bob And they'd rather see her than me.

Chris Apparently.

A slight moment

Bob Why didn't you say before?

Chris She only telephoned this morning—I forgot to tell you.

Bob Yeah—well—it's not that important, is it?

It's a bad moment for both of them. She knows she has turned the knife, but can't stop it. But she makes the nearest attempt she can, with:

Chris D'you want a cup of tea or something before you go?

Bob No thanks.

Chris Suit yourself. I'm having one. (*She moves to the door*)

Bob Were *you* any different?

She turns

Once you had a mug like me to support *you*?

Chris (*quietly*) I stopped working because that's what you wanted. You wanted me here, looking after you.

Bob I don't remember you protesting too much.

Chris No. No, I didn't protest at all. For whatever reason, I decided that my work was *here*. Not that it's proper work, of course it isn't—not like *your* work—Ssshhh—now now, darling, Daddy's working—Daddy's having a rest, we mustn't disturb him. But any time *you* wanted attention, any time the kids were in trouble, Mummy was always available. No matter what she's doing, Mummy must be available. Daddy earns the money . . . Mummy pays the bill.

Bob (*clumsily*) Yeah—well—that's down to both of us.

He turns away from her. This moment. And then, as though speaking her thoughts aloud:

Chris I tried for a job. Last week. Nothing much—just some temping in a local office, but I thought—at least it . . . I sat there, at the interview—and I couldn't speak. I felt totally inadequate. Totally lacking in confidence. I was on my own—and I was afraid. And for that—I blame you.

Chris goes out

For a moment he stands. Then, as he pulls out a folded letter, the Lights change to bright lighting DS. *He indicates the letter to the audience, and reads:*

Bob "Just a note to say that the Court has informed me that the matter has been set down for trial and that there should be a hearing date issued shortly. I will let you know the date as soon as I am informed of it. In the meantime, may I take it that the situation between your wife and yourself is reasonably amicable?" (*He looks up at the audience*) Now there's a funny thing . . . there's a funny thing . . . (*Like a comedian. But he becomes dejected again, pocketing the letter as:*)

The Lights change to evening lighting

Diana enters. She wears her glasses and carries a book—she's been doing her accounts. She smiles, but nervously. He's late home and she feels insecure

(*Excessively bright*) Hi!

Diana (*sitting*) I didn't think you were coming back.

Bob Di——

Diana You said you'd phone on the way.

Bob There wasn't a box that was working. Going into a phone box nowadays is like visiting an electronic slaughterhouse. Dial nine-nine-nine? You're lucky if you can find the bloody dial.

He kisses her brow. The moment has eased. She stands

Diana I'll get you something to eat.

Bob Umm ... no it's all right thanks, I'm—er—I'm not hungry.

Diana You mean you've eaten. (*The inference loud and clear*)

Bob I had a *sandwich*. (*He slumps into the chair*)

Diana You don't want anything then.

Bob (*a sudden flash of irritation*) Why do you have to *provide* all the time?

This moment

Just a cup of coffee then I want to get on with some work—and I'll make the coffee myself—believe it or not, I'm actually capable.

A slight moment

Diana Fine. (*She makes to go out, but*)

Bob Look—I'm sorry—I just want to finish off that storyline. They were nagging me again this morning.

Diana Do you have to do it tonight?

Bob I do if I want to keep several wolves from several doors.

She makes to go out, but:

Diana Oh yes—Robin phoned—to see if you wanted to play golf tomorrow.

Bob No, I don't think so.

Diana Do you good.

Bob No, I'm off golf at the minute. I don't enjoy it. Dunno why: maybe it's my age. Maybe I'm going through the change of swing.

Again she is about to go out, but:

Diana And you said to remind you about seeing your mother some time this week.

Bob (*puffing out air*) Oh ... I dunno ... Thursday.

Diana You're seeing your accountant Thursday.

Bob Eh?

Diana About seeing the taxman next Wednesday.

Bob Oh, Christ, yeah. Friday then.

Diana We're taking Sasha to that concert on Friday.

Bob That what?

Diana The school concert. You said you'd——

Bob Yeah, yeah. I dunno ... (*again the flash of irritation*) ... I *dunno*. Yeah—well—I'll sort something out.

She almost goes out, but:

Diana I know what you're going to say—but you really can't keep putting it off.
Bob Putting what off?
Diana Telling your mother.
Bob She's my mother—I'll tell her when I'm ready—OK?

Diana goes out

He gets up and crosses to take up the cordless telephone. As he dials the Lights change to bright lighting DS *and he addresses the audience:*

My mother . . . my mother is a terrible cook. She's only once in her life produced a decent meal and my father—my father—wouldn't let anyone touch it until he'd got this bloke round to take a coloured photograph.

Christine and Diana enter

Bob sits on the sofa and the two women sit, one each side of him, as the Lights focus on the sofa

Why do I lie to her? Why does she make me feel guilty all the time?
Diana He thinks he's Jewish.
Chris It's psychosemitic.
Bob (*brightly, into the telephone*) Hello Mum.

All three are looking straight ahead as:

Diana Who's that?
Bob Who do you think it is—it's your son.
Chris (*lifelessly*) Oh hello son, how are you?
Bob I'm fine—fine—how are *you*?
Diana Oh, not so good, son—still—mustn't grumble.
Chris But she will—she will.
Diana I've been worried about you.
Bob Why's that?
Chris I never hear from you.
Diana It never occurs to her to phone *him*.
Chris I said to your Aunt Lily . . .
Diana Something's happened to that boy.
Chris You mark my words.
Bob Yeah, I'm sorry, Mum—I've been up to my eyes.
Chris I quite understand, son.
Diana Your work must come first.
Bob (*taking the bull by the horns*) Mum—listen—there's something I've got to tell you.
Chris Even then he lied.
Bob Things haven't been going so well. At home. I thought it best—for the sake of everyone—if I moved out. Just for a few days—no rows or anything—it's all perfectly—you know. Nothing permanent—just until we—you know. And that's about it, really, Mum.

A moment and then:

Ten nine eight seven lift-off.

And he leans back in the sofa, still as though using the telephone, and the two women lean forward and—very fast:

Diana I knew it.
Chris I said to your Aunt Lily ...
Diana Lily I said ...
Chris That boy's unhappy ...
Diana I said ...
Chris He's been unhappy ...
Diana For a long time ...
Chris Surprised?
Diana How can I be ...
Chris Surprised.
Diana You think...
Chris A mother ...
Diana Doesn't know?
Chris I'm only glad ...
Diana Your poor dear father ...
Chris Isn't alive to hear this.
Diana She's never really looked after you ...
Chris Has she, son?
Diana Not like a wife.
Chris Oh those poor dear children.
Diana Are you eating?
Chris What about your washing?
Diana }
Chris } (*together*) I worry about you.
Chris I can't help it, son.
Diana It's only natural.
Diana }
Chris } (*together*) I'm your mother

The two women exit quickly

Bob leans forward and, into the telephone:

Bob No thanks, Mum—nothing—honestly. You've done enough already.

The Lights change to evening lighting. He puts down the telephone and slumps on the sofa as though exhausted, pulling out a handkerchief to mop his brow as:

Chris enters, carrying a newspaper and her glasses

He pats his chest to show how winded he is and smiles, with:

They tire me out.

She sits in the easy chair and appears to be more interested in the paper as:

Chris You shouldn't roll about all over the floor with them then, should
you?

Bob Oh come on Chris—they enjoy it.

Chris They get over-tired and they won't sleep.

A moment

Bob Anyway—how are you?

Chris (*reading*) Fine. How are *you*?

Bob Not so bad. Got a cold coming, I think.

Chris Why? Isn't she looking after you?

A moment. And, with an attempt at light conversation:

Bob Are you going out at all?

Chris When I'm asked.

Bob Not that bad, is it? I mean, there's——

Chris You try being a woman on your own.

A moment. He makes another attempt

Bob Anyway. I think they had a nice day.

Chris Where did you take them?

Bob We didn't go anywhere really . . . had a walk along the river . . . came
back . . . they watched the telly. You know.

Chris I thought the idea was for you to take them out.

Bob I can't take them out all the time, Chris—you don't know what it's like,
trolling round the streets, trying to think of somewhere to go, stuffing
them full of burgers and milk shakes . . . apart from anything else, I never
get the chance to talk to them.

Chris You talk to them better when they're watching television, do you?

A moment

Bob He didn't eat much.

Chris He hasn't eaten much all week.

Bob No. We had roast beef and he hardly touched it. Loulie shovelled it
away as usual——

Chris You can afford roast beef, can you?

Bob Can't you?

Chris Not any more—no.

A moment. Pointless arguing about money again

Bob Anyway . . . (*he manages a little smile*) . . . what have *you* done today?

Chris What I always do—clear this place up.

Bob I thought you might have—you know—had a rest or something.

*She puts the paper on the floor, takes off her glasses and for the first time looks
directly at him as:*

Chris Does it ever occur to you that they'd rather see you on your own?

Bob They've never said anything.

Chris Have you ever asked them?

Bob Yes I have.
Chris Liar.
Bob Yeah—all right—I'm a liar.
Chris They don't like her.
Bob That's not the way it——
Chris They don't like the way she keeps touching you.
Bob She doesn't keep——
Chris You should have more sense.
Bob Been asking questions, have you?
Chris I don't have to.
Bob You mean they report back.
Chris That's right.
Bob *Why?*
Chris Because they obviously don't like it, that's why, you insensitive sod.

A moment

Taking them round to that place—you ought to have more sense.
Bob I do what I think is best for them.
Chris You do what you think is best for *you*. All I ever hear is how rough it
is for you. Have you ever once stopped to consider what it's like for me?
When they come back here after being with Daddy and his tart? What
sort of mood d'you think they're in when you walk out of that door? Have
you ever tried to stop the tears? And who do you think gets the blame for
it all—eh? You're so busy being sensitive you can't see an inch in front of
your sodding face. (*And suddenly she is standing and all her attempt at
control is gone as:*) I'm not having a woman like that influencing my
children. They're my children, not hers, and they always will be.
Bob ("*patiently*") What are you trying to say, Chris?
Chris I don't want them round that house.
Bob Where am I supposed to take them?
Chris That's your problem.
Bob Look—as soon as this bloody divorce comes through I'll be entitled to
have those kids two weekends a month——
Chris Yes, well, we'll see about that, won't we?
Bob (*losing his temper*) All right! You go and see your solicitor . . . tell him
I'm a bad influence . . . you want to make things difficult, you go ahead
and do it . . . you do it, Chris . . . and then you'll find out just how bloody
difficult *I* can be.

*He has been advancing towards her, his voice and manner threatening so that
for a moment she feels that he might strike her, but:*

Chris Don't you think I'm entitled to worry about them?
Bob Don't you think *I* worry?
Chris You've never worried about them before.
Bob Why don't you *think* before you say something like that.
Chris Well did you?
Bob No, no—I'm a lousy bloody father.

Chris Do you think you're a good one? After what you've done? What sort
of father is that?

A moment. Both very subdued now, as:

Bob Yes ... well ... I'll phone them tomorrow then.
Chris Not before seven—they've got their piano lesson.
Bob Oh yeah—I've got to give you a cheque, haven't I?
Chris End of the month will do.
Bob (*nodding*) And I'll be over on Wednesday.
Chris It's up to you.

*And she makes to exit, but stands in the doorway, facing the audience as the
Lights change, dimming* US *and with a spot on Chris. With a sudden burst of
energy, Bob goes to the unfinished shelf unit, takes up a tin of clear varnish and
a brush ... and begins varnishing. He does it fiercely, his mind full of anger*

Bob (*muttering to himself*) It's hopeless trying to talk to her ...
Chris That's right. I'm too stupid.
Bob On and on and ...
Chris That's his favourite word for me. Stupid.
Bob *Stupid.*
Chris What was it he used to say to his fancy friends? "Wait until you meet
her—she's so refreshingly uncomplicated."
Bob Rubbish.
Chris "A good solid Northern lass without an ounce of pretention." How
long did that last? How long before the passion wore off and the good
solid Northern lass stopped being uncomplicated and started being
stupid?
Bob *Stupid.*
Chris Not so wonderful then, was it? All he's ever seen me as is an extension
of himself. So if *I'm* stupid ...

She smiles flatly at the audience and goes out as:

Diana enters as the Lights change to evening light

*She is much aware of his angry mood. He doesn't respond to her entrance. She
sits, taking up the papers left behind by Chris, attempts to read, but:*

Diana D'you want to talk about it?
Bob No.

*She lets it rest, knowing that he won't. He continues jabbing at the woodwork
for a moment and then stops, with:*

The cow. Why did I marry her? (*Another couple of jabs with the brush,
but:*) D'you mind if I pack this in? I'm jiggered.
Diana No of course I don't mind, I thought you——
Bob I am, I'm jiggered. (*He puts down the tin, moves to slump on the sofa. A
moment*) She was always laughing. Always smiling. Always had only one
face for the world. Dead straight. Honest. I can't remember the last time I
saw her smile. Not really smile. Which is down to me, isn't it? (*A moment*)

She's not a bad woman. She really isn't. (*A moment*) I've never known her so depressed.

A moment. Then Diana gets up and starts unnecessarily tidying up the newspapers

Diana It's only to be expected, isn't it?
Bob Not that she'd say as much. Too bloody proud.
Diana That's what you call it, is it—proud?
Bob What's that supposed to mean?
Diana All you ever do is——
Bob Is what?
Diana It doesn't matter——
Bob Is *what*?

A moment. She makes a big effort to remain calm as:

Diana All you ever do is to make excuses for her. Has she ever once—just once—admitted any responsibility at all for what's happened?
Bob I see.
Diana No you don't see. There are two of you, for God's sake. It can't all be your fault.
Bob I'm not saying it is all my——
Diana But you do. Why can't you behave as the situation dictates—not just to satisfy your ego?

This moment. Then:

Bob ("*patiently*") I left her didn't I? (*He moves to the shelf unit and takes up the tin of varnish and brush, so that his back is towards us*)
Diana Every time you go there, you come back in the same mood ... of course she's going to be funny about the children, of course she's going to argue about money ... she's hurt and they're the only things she's got to hurt you back with ...
Bob I know, I know ...
Diana Well if you know it, stop fighting about it and get it done through a solicitor ... it's what they're for, for God's sake.
Bob You're right, you're absolutely right ...
Diana Do you ever stop to think what it does to her, seeing you there? You're supposed to be seeing the children, not mowing the lawn and everything else you do.
Bob I know her, Di: I know the things she can't do.
Diana Why can't she?
Bob All right—won't.
Diana Because you've never let her—and as long as she knows that—as long as she knows you think that——
Bob That's not the way her mind works.
Diana It is the way her mind works: believe me, I know.

This moment. And she gathers herself for what she really wants to say, and:

But if you think your marriage has got a hope in hell ...

Bob You mean go back.

Diana If that's what you want, if that's what you really want—yes.

Bob You'd like that, would you?

Diana No, I would not like it. But if you really think it's worth at try . . . if you really think she's so bloody hard done by and it's all your fault then give it a try . . . go back . . . but *do* it.

This moment. She is close to giving way and is desperately trying not to. He makes to move to her but she turns away and remains with her back to him as:

I mean it, Bob, I really mean it. Because I just can't . . . (*And again she stops and gathers herself and:*) I'm not responsible for what happened between you and your wife. You want me to be, but I'm not. I'm responsible only for what happens between you and me and if you can't accept that . . . You see . . . I was aware of the problems and I thought I could cope and now I find I'm not as strong as I want to be . . . (*She stops. A moment*)

Bob Yes.

This moment. He returns to varnishing the shelves

Diana I shall have to leave early in the morning.

He nods

So if you could make sure Sasha has an egg or something.

Bob Right.

Diana And run her to school.

Bob Right.

Diana Oh—and she mustn't forget to take that form.

Bob Right.

Diana Perhaps I should leave her a note.

Bob No, I'll tell her.

Diana You're sure?

Bob OK—leave her a note. You'll both be happier.

This moment. Then she moves to the door but:

Diana Are you coming up?

Bob Just finish this.

A moment

Diana Come to bed.

Bob Yes, all *right*, Chris.

A moment as they both realize what he has said

I just want to finish this—OK?

A moment

She goes out

The Lights change to bright lighting DS, *as Bob takes out a letter, indicates it to the audience as he addresses them with:*

They love letters, solicitors. Charge you by the word. (*He reads*) "I have now received notification that your case is set down for hearing on the twentieth November at ten p.m." (*He looks up*) What he means is ten a.m. They make these deliberate mistakes to prove you're still alive and capable of passing over five pound notes. (*He reads*) "You, of course, will not be required to attend." (*He pockets the letter*) You, of course, will not be required to attend. (*A flat smile*) The only time she cried was when the dog died. Yeah, the dog. A week before D Day. I dunno ... it was just about all she needed, I suppose.

The Lights change — dim evening light

> *Christine enters. She looks tired, lifeless. She moves to the coffee table and takes up her cigarettes. Finds the box of matches empty*

Bob moves to her, lights her cigarette with his lighter. Then he holds out the lighter for her to take. A moment. And she takes it with a slight smile. They sit, Christine on the sofa, Bob in the chair as:

Chris It wasn't so much the operation as the anaesthetic apparently. A dog that age. As ill as she was. He said it was two to one against. I was on pins all day. Anyway ... four o'clock ... he phoned ... and that was that.

A moment

Bob Poor old girl, eh?

A moment

How did the kids take it?
Chris They both cried of course. They don't want another one — not a dog.

A moment

Bob I remember bringing her home — inside my coat. Loulie must have been — what, about three months.

A moment

Chris Jamie says he wants a horse. If he can't have a horse he'll have a budgerigar.

Bob manages a little smile

Bob Practical, you see. Like his mother.
Chris Anyway. It'll cost about forty quid. That's for the operation and the stuff they gave her beforehand.
Bob Yeah — well — let me have the bill and — you know. (*A moment*) I think you should have another dog ... you know — being on your own, house this size. On the other hand ... it might be cheaper to give the guinea pig judo lessons.

A moment

Chris I'm sorry.
Bob What for?

Chris More money for you to pay out.
Bob Don't be daft—of course I'll pay it.

She looks at him directly for the first time and, still wearily:

Chris You really have got yourself into a mess, haven't you?

A moment. He gives a sort of shrug

Bob Yeah. Well ...
Chris You're such a bloody fool.

A moment

Bob Chris ... If I thought there was a hope in hell of us getting together
   again——
Chris No-one's asking you to come back.
Bob No. No-one's asking. And that's it, you see. Not once—not once in this
   whole lousy business have you——
Chris You wanted your freedom. Well—you've got it, haven't you?

A moment. He puts a hand to his brow, fingers it wearily

   What's up? Isn't she as wonderful as you thought she was?

A moment

Bob Yeah ... well ... it's pointless going through all that again.
Chris Did it never occur to you that we don't want you back?
Bob What d'you mean—we?
Chris The kids.
Bob What are you trying to say?
Chris Maybe they're more resilient than you give them credit for.
Bob I hope they are.
Chris They took a vote on it.
Bob On what?
Chris Whether they want you back.
Bob And?
Chris One abstention, one don't know.
Bob Yeah—well—that's me—the popular man of the people.

A moment

   They didn't did they?

*She looks at him. And smiles ... and the smile becomes a chuckle ... and the
chuckle becomes tears ... tears for the whole wretched situation. She tries to
fight them back, not wanting him to see. He sits watching her hopelessly. Close
to tears himself ... and goes to her, tries to put his arms around her with:*

   Chris ...

But she pulls away

Chris No ... leave me alone ... please.

A moment. Then he moves away. This moment . . . him standing . . . her crying quietly, desperately. And then, softly:

Bob Christ . . . you're so bloody *stubborn*.

Chris Why couldn't you have been like the rest of them? Why couldn't you have had your fun and kept your mouth shut? No . . . not you . . . you have to get involved . . . you have to get bloody *involved*.

Bob Chris . . .

Chris Go way . . . please . . . go away.

A moment. And he turns away from her. She remains sitting, looking down at her clenched hands

The Lights change—bright lighting DS

Bob (*to the audience*) Come the big day . . . I nearly sent her some flowers. I mean, what do you do after twelve years? A Divorceogram? As it turned out . . . nothing.

Christine gets up and wearily moves to the door, calling:

Chris Yes . . . all right . . . all right! What? Do you know what time it is? Stop arguing, for God's sake stop arguing!

She goes out

Bob And that . . . was it. Next week, I was over seeing the kids as though——

Diana enters with:

Diana As though it hadn't happened.

Bob Which in a way . . . I should have stayed away. I mean . . . common-sense.

The Lights change—general lighting, as he turns to Diana who has sat in the chair to sew a button on to a child's shirt. Immediately he assumes brightness as he kisses her brow and sits on the sofa

Diana How was it?

Bob Fine. Jamie wasn't there—football practice. Loulie made us some cakes—she gave me some to bring back.

Diana That was nice of her.

Bob I ate them on the way here—I knew you wouldn't mind, I was starving. Anyway, next time she comes over, tell her how nice they were, will you?

A moment

Diana I spent most of the afternoon trying to get Sasha's passport.

Bob Oh yeah?

Diana You don't remember, do you?

Bob Of course I remember—something about—where is it . . .?

Diana Her father's taking her to Amsterdam at half-term.

Bob Yeah, well, she'll like that, won't she? (*Said with the minimum of enthusiasm*)

Diana Do you know she tried to tell you about it last night?

Bob Not to my knowledge she——

Diana She asked you if you'd ever been there.

Bob I didn't hear her.

Diana No. No, you didn't hear her. She went bright red. I've never seen her so embarrassed, I thought she was going to cry.

Bob I don't deliberately ignore her for Chrissake . . .

Diana I'm not saying you do.

Bob What am I supposed to do? Most of the time she ignores me and when I do speak to her she argues with me all the time.

Diana She doesn't ignore you.

Bob Oh come off it, Di—you're so bloody protective.

Diana Does it ever occur to you that sometimes the look on your face is enough to put anyone off—let alone a nine-year-old child?

Bob You've always got an excuse for her.

Diana Don't you make excuses for your children?

Bob I haven't got my children.

Diana Is that my fault?

Bob No. Nothing's your fault, is it, Di?

A moment. She moves to the door

Diana I'm going to have a bath.

Bob Di . . . look, I'm sorry. You're quite right—I'm not very good with her. I try, but . . . I always feel you're looking over my shoulder. I always feel it's . . . you and her and . . . me.

Diana That's not true.

Bob Whether it's true or not—it's what I *think*. Just . . . give me a hand, eh?

Diana It's not a hand you need, Bob. It's a lap to sit on.

She goes out

Bob (*making to go after her*) Now wait a minute . . .

But Christine enters

Chris I thought you said you'd be here at three.

Bob Yes—well—as a matter of fact I've been to the doctor.

Chris What was it this time?

Bob There's a—lump under my arm.

Chris What did he say?

Bob (*hesitating, but*) It's the deodorant I'm using.

Chris Deodorant?

Bob Apparently it's pretty common nowadays.

Chris That must have disappointed you.

Bob For people with delicate skins.

Chris He should examine your behind—it's like a bloody elephant's.

Bob What happens is that the deodorant bungs up the pores and you get this lump.

Chris I suppose you thought it was cancer.

Bob Why should I think it's cancer?

Chris Because you always think it's cancer.

Bob That's not true.

Chris Come off it: ever since your father died.

Bob Can I tell you something? If I'm gonna go, I'll go with something a bit more romantic than cancer of the armpit.

Chris Oh yes—of course—you're very strong on romance, aren't you? (*A "polite" smile*) Now will you please get on with my shelves?

And she goes out quickly

Diana enters with:

Diana D'you want anything before I go up?

Bob No thanks—look—Di—about half-term—Chris is taking the kids up to her mother for the week.

Diana Yes, you said—Well?

Bob Well the thing is . . . I said I'd look after the house.

Diana What d'you mean—look after it?

Bob Well—you know—with those flats being built next door—the place is wide open.

Diana What d'you mean—look after it?

Bob I said I'd move in—just for the week.

Diana I see.

Bob Well apart from anything else, there's the dog.

Diana What about the dog?

Bob Well someone's got to look after it.

Diana Bring it here.

Bob No—that's the whole point—I mean, that's why I bought another dog—it's supposed to be looking after the house.

Diana So you look after the dog and the dog looks after the house.

Bob You know what I mean.

Diana No I don't bloody well know what you mean . . . for God's sake . . . either you're divorced from her or you're not.

Bob It doesn't mean to say I can't help her.

Diana Help her? I'm surprised you don't filter the air she breathes.

Bob Yeah, yeah, all right.

Diana Did *she* suggest it?

Bob Yes.

Diana Liar.

Diana exits

Bob Shit. Shit shit *shit*.

Christine enters with a dustpan and brush

Chris That's right, lose your temper.

Bob I am not losing my temper.

Chris You've finished for today, have you?

Bob Yes.

Chris I can start clearing up then, can I?

Bob (*taking up his bag*) I still can't find my chisel.

Chris What chisel?

Bob My half-inch chisel.

Chris The one *I* bought you?

Bob Good chisel, that is.

Chris You're not accusing me, are you?

Bob I'm not accusing anyone.

Chris Perhaps *she's* got it.

Bob What would she want with a half-inch chisel?

Chris I don't know: some of the things I've heard about her.

Bob You've never met her.

Chris No and I don't want to.

Christine exits as:

Diana enters to stand in the doorway. She is rubbing her hands together

Diana I mean, what else are you going to do? You see the children every weekend, you see them twice during the week, you phone every day—spending most of the time talking to *her*—you do the garden, you fix the plumbing, you make the shelves, you pay for everything including the hairdresser, you've even taken her to the *dentist.*

Bob *Once.*

Diana Why even once?

Bob You know perfectly well—she was having an anaesthetic and they wanted someone to drive her home.

Diana Hasn't she got any friends?

Bob There was no one available.

Diana Then she should have hired a car.

Bob It was cheaper for me to do it.

Diana *She* should pay for it!

Bob All right! But it all comes back to me in the long run, doesn't it?

Diana I mean, it's ridiculous ... she goes to the theatre and I find myself asking if she's had a good time. What the hell should *I* care if she's had a good time?

Bob What are you afraid of?

Diana Why should I be——

Bob (*miming*) All this wringing the hands bit.

Diana I am not wringing my hands with fear ... I'm wringing them because I've just put some hand-cream on. Which I bought myself. (*And she stands in the doorway, looking at him, rubbing her hands together as:*)

Christine enters

The Lights change to bright lighting DS

Chris And tell your tart to stop mauling my kids.

Bob (*wearily*) Will you please stop calling her my tart.

Chris Tell your significant other person to stop mauling my kids—OK?

Bob She doesn't maul them.

Chris Running round after them all the time ... you're not trying to tell me she likes them.

Bob Of course she likes them—they're my kids.

Chris (*mimicking*) Of course she likes them—you're her meal ticket. Well you can tell her from me—she can have you and good riddance—but she's not having my kids . . .

Diana It's just an excuse, isn't it?

Bob What is?

Diana Everything you do. You've got to be needed. You've got to be "the man".

Bob There's nothing wrong in—in trying to maintain a relationship.

Diana
Chris (*together*) Relationship?

Diana You don't want a relationship.

Chris You couldn't *have* a relationship.

Diana All you want is the belief that a relationship exists.

The two women advance towards him so that they are standing on either side of him throughout:

Bob *Chris.*

Diana You see?

Bob *Di.*

Diana Thank you.

Bob You've got to trust me.

Diana (*hard*) The sink's blocked up.

Bob What do you mean—the sink's blocked up?

Diana What I say—the sink's blocked up.

Chris It's been blocked up for three days.

Bob Why don't you get someone *in*?

Diana (*as though to a child*) I said I'd get someone in . . .

Chris But you said "no no" you said . . .

Diana "I'll do it" . . .

Chris Or don't you remember that either?

Bob If I said I'd do it, I'll do it.

Diana If you can find your tools.

Chris I'd give her a ring.

Diana I'm sure she'll know where they are.

Bob Very sharp, very witty.

Diana You want me to trust you—all right, I trust you.

Chris All I want *you* to do is fix the sink. Not for me. For you.

Diana So that you can use your wonderful working-class hands and feel at peace with the world.

Chris Is it a saw?

Diana Is it a plane?

Chris
Diana (*together*) It's Maintenance Man!

Bob Anyway . . . what d'you mean—"she"?

Diana *Her.*

Bob She's got a name, y'know.

Chris Oh yes—she's got a name all right.

Bob I'm *living* with her. We've been divorced for six months for Chrissake.
You've got to stop talking about her like she's . . .

Diana I don't want to talk about her . . .

Chris I don't want to see her, I don't want to speak to her.

Diana I don't want to know anything about her.

Chris If you want to come here . . .

Diana If you want to *do* things . . .

Chris *Do it.*

Diana But don't keep ramming her down my throat.

Chris I don't want to know.

Diana I don't want to *know.*

Bob What *do* you want for Chrissake!

Chris What do we want?

Diana What do women want?

Chris Whatever it is . . .

Diana ⎱ (*together*) We can't have it.
Chris ⎰

Bob I don't know where I am!

Chris Don't you?

Diana Don't you really?

Chris If you're thinking of having a nervous breakdown . . .

Diana Forget it.

Diana ⎱ (*together*) You haven't got the time.
Chris ⎰

Diana and Christine exit

Bob turns to the audience, bewildered

Bob What chance have we got? We're doomed . . . doomed from the minute
we're born . . . doomed from the minute we blink up into a pair of bloody
great boobs. Wouldn't we have more chance if the first thing we saw was a
pair of braces and a Capstan Full Strength? Which . . . as readers of the
old Picturegoer might say . . . is where I came in. I'm here . . . (*but
suddenly, more brightly*) . . . but suddenly . . . the cloud has a silver
lifeboat.

The Lights change to daylight, as:

*Christine enters. She carries a bowl of flowers which she puts down on a
table. She looks more relaxed than we've seen her before, has her hair done
differently*

When d'you start?

Chris Next week.

Bob That's great—I mean—terrific.

Chris The money won't be up to much—part-time three days a week. (*She
sits on the sofa*)

Bob It's not just the money though, is it? It's getting you out of yourself
more than anything. I am, I'm really pleased.

And he obviously is. She smiles at him

Chris And you're all right, are you?
Bob Me? I'm fine. (*But he can't resist*) Got to go to the hospital next week.
Chris What for?
Bob I keep getting these pains in my fingers. (*He sits next to her, extending his hand*)

And, almost without realizing it, she finds herself taking hold of his hand. It's the first time she's actually touched him for months. And they are both very much aware of it: aware of the somehow strange intimacy of it. This moment. Then he withdraws the hand with:

They're gonna do some tests. Touch of rheumatism I reckon. Probably give me some heat treatment or something.

And suddenly she is smiling to herself. He finds himself smiling back with:

Let's have it then.
Chris I was thinking ... you've got an aerosol spray for every part of your body.
Bob More or less, I suppose.
Chris You remember that time you went away on that golfing weekend with Des , ..
Bob (*here it comes*) Oh yes ...?
Chris He said when you collected up your aerosols in the bathroom it sounded like Napoleon's army on the march.
Bob Yes—well—he would, wouldn't he—Des.

All lightly, fondly ... closer than we've seen them

And—er—it's still OK for me to have the kids this weekend.
Chris Why don't you keep them until Monday morning? You could take them straight to school ...
Bob If you're sure you——
Chris They'd like that.

A slight moment

Bob As long as you don't——
Chris Really. I'd like you to have them.

A moment

Bob OK—I'll pick them up Friday then.
Chris Why don't we have a cup of tea before you go?
Bob Er ... (*he smiles*) ... thanks.

She moves to the door, but:

Chris I don't want to argue any more, Bob. I really don't.

And she goes out

The Lights change to dim lighting—evening—lamp R *on*

A moment. And Diana enters, wearing a topcoat. She moves across to drop his car keys into his hand, with:

Bob How much did you give him?
Diana Four pounds fifty.

He grimaces, then jerks a thumb towards the shelf units

Bob He's been at the whisky again.
Diana Poor Julian. (*She sits next to him, still in the topcoat*)
Bob Poor nothing.

He puts an arm around her. She rests her head against him

Diana Not a bad film though, was it?
Bob Film was all right. The audience was terrible.
Diana Mmm.
Bob How about that woman?
Diana (*smiling*) "Excuse me, madam, do you mind removing your crash helmet?"
Bob Well I couldn't see anything.
Diana You didn't have to knock on it.
Bob She couldn't hear with those great leather things hanging down. (*A moment*) Haven't been to the pictures for ages, have we? (*He kisses her on the cheek. A moment*) I'm really pleased about Chris.
Diana (*genuinely*) Yes. I know.
Bob It can't be easy for her. But she's really making an effort. She looked really pretty yesterday, you know. Had her hair done differently and everything. She did—she looked really pretty.

A moment

It hasn't been easy for you, either. But it's gonna be all right, Di. I know it is.

A moment. Then she kisses him and:

Diana I love you.

He smiles up at her as she stands, reaching out to touch her hand

She goes out, taking off her coat

A moment. The Lights change to daylight. Then he frowns—something in the sofa is digging into him. He reaches under the cushion to take out a half-inch chisel. Gives a little jerk of the head, puts the chisel on the coffee table and digs beneath the cushion to see what else he can find. He pulls out a child's skate. Spins the wheels. One of them jams. He takes a screwdriver from the box on the coffee table and is adjusting the wheel when:

Christine enters

They exchange smiles. She sits in the armchair, she chooses her moment

Chris I'm thinking of taking the kids to Bournemouth for the weekend.

Bob That's nice.

Chris You know—just a couple of days' break.

Bob Do you good. (*He continues mending the skate as:*) What will you do—stay in a hotel?

Chris Yes, I think so.

Bob Tell you what—I'll ring up—book a room.

Chris No, no, that's fine.

Bob No trouble.

Chris No—really.

Bob (*nodding*) How are you off for cash?

Chris No, that's all right. (*After a pause*) We're being taken.

A moment. She is aware of the effect it will have

Bob Uh-huh.

Chris We're going with Charles.

This moment. Then—with an exaggerated drawl:

Bob Charles?

Chris Yes. That Charles.

A slight moment

Bob Very nice.

A slight moment

You've—er—you've been seeing something of him, have you?

Chris He phoned one night—invited me out to dinner. I've been seeing him ever since.

Bob Yeah ... well ... that's good ... he's—you know—I like old Charles.

Chris He's good with the kids and everything.

Bob They haven't said anything.

Chris I asked them not to.

This moment. He is momentarily thrown. But can't resist, although trying to make light of it:

Bob He's a bit old though, isn't he, Chris?

Chris He's forty-nine.

Bob I mean—you know—how long is it since his wife died?

Chris I like him, Bob. I can talk to him.

Bob Yeah—well—as long as you can talk to him.

A moment. And suddenly he is standing and indicating the shelves as:

You mean all the time I was coming round here, putting up those shelves and everything, you were seeing him?

Chris You would have been disappointed.

Bob How d'you mean—disappointed?

Chris I mean not doing things for me.

He looks at her, not knowing whether to laugh or cry

Bob That's great, that is ... that's bloody great. (*He shakes his head in disbelief, and:*) Not that it's any of my business—but you're not saying you're going to marry him, are you?

Chris No. (*After a slight pause*) I don't know. (*She stands*) All I know is—I don't have to depend on you any more. Not because of him, because of me. I'd like to think I didn't have to depend on any man—but I don't think I'm made that way. You'll always be part of my life of course. Because of the children. But it doesn't end with you. I'm sorry. It really doesn't.

She goes out, closing the door

He stands for a moment; stunned, and then calls:

Bob Di ...

Diana enters, reading one of her work books

He sits on the sofa and she sits in the chair as:

Diana Mmm? (*She looks at the book*)
Bob I reckon we should buy a bigger house.
Diana (*looking up at him*) How d'you mean—a bigger house?
Bob I'm thinking of the kids more than anything—we'll obviously be seeing a lot more of my two—I'd like to think they could spread out a bit—have a room each—somewhere they can call their own. And Sasha of course.

A moment

Diana You mean buy it together.
Bob Well—yes—I mean—if you sold this place and put some of that down as a deposit—I'd do the rest. What d'you think?

A moment

Diana No.

He tries on a smile

Bob Why not?

A moment

Diana Because I love you. Because the only way I think I can make it work is by not committing myself to you. By not having you committing yourself to *me*.
Bob That's bloody daft: of course I'm committed to you—I've asked you to marry me.
Diana And I said no.
Bob You said not yet.
Diana And now I'm saying no.
Bob Why?
Diana I love you and I want to stay with you. But I won't marry you. (*She gets up, moving to the door, but:*) Perhaps commitment's the wrong word.

(*She smiles faintly*) It usually is with me. I won't depend on you. You ask for it—but you don't really want it. Do you?

She touches his head gently and then goes out, closing the door

He looks at the audience, wanting to say something. But nothing will come. A moment. Then he takes up the telephone and dials. He stands and paces a little, waiting for it to be answered, and:

Bob (*brightly*) Hello darling, it's Daddy. What's been happening with *you* today? . . . Oh I see . . . it's on now, is it? . . . No, of course I don't mind—is Jamie there? . . . No, no—not if he's watching it too—just send him my love. Is Mummy there? . . . Can I have a word? . . . All right darling, I love you. (*It is clear that his daughter has quickly put the receiver down before he finished telling her he loves her. But he brightens again as:*) Hello Chris . . . . So Loulie says . . . I always seem to phone at the wrong time, don't I? . . . Oh, sorry, I'll let you get on then. . . . No, no, just wanted to say hello. . . . Yes, I'm fine, terrific. I'll phone tomorrow then. 'Bye. (*A moment. He puts the telephone quickly down on to the coffee table. Looks at the audience and, slowly, seriously:*) What I wanted to tell her was . . . you see . . . I went for these tests at the hospital. Sorry to have to tell you this, they said . . . but your blood group has been discontinued. (*He smiles flatly . . . then turns to regard the unfinished shelf unit. Suddenly galvanized into action, he moves the low table, puts a plank of wood across it, takes out his saw. These movements punctuated by the following speech to the audience*) Oh yes . . . I've got a new secretary. Well, I call her a secretary, she types my scripts— part-time—you know. Just had the big bust-up with her fellah so she's moved into this little flat in Parson's Green.

The Lights begin to dim slowly. He makes to saw, but:

Pretty little thing, she is. Or would be, if she stopped crying herself to sleep every night. She—er—she was asking me how you put cork tiles on the wall. I said if you hang on a bit I'll give you a hand. Well . . . she's on her own and everything . . . you've got to, haven't you?

And he begins sawing . . . and then humming cheerfully to himself as——

the CURTAIN *falls*

FURNITURE AND PROPERTY LIST

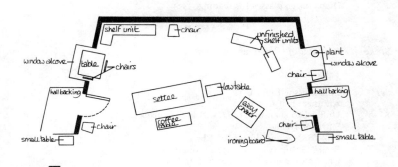

ACT I

On stage: Table. *On it:* radio, vase of flowers
6 dining chairs
Sofa. *On it:* cushions
Easy chair
Coffee table. *On it:* cordless telephone, ashtray, box containing items including a screwdriver, box of matches, empty cigarette packet
Low table. *On it:* length of wood, saw, tape measure, pencil, carpenter's square. *Underneath it:* newspaper, toolbag and tools scattered around including cordless drill (practical), sandpaper
Ironing board. *On it:* iron, half-finished tablecloth. *Near it:* pile of completed ironing
Wooden shelf unit. *On it:* books, odds and ends
Unfinished wooden shelf unit, shelves, wood
2 small tables. *On each:* a lamp
In alcove L: clean shirt, deodorant spray, jacket, tie, breath freshner spray, raincoat with lighter in pocket
General evidence of children, various plants
Carpet
Window curtains (open)

Off stage: M & S bag containing food, men's socks, girl's cardigan, panties, car keys
             (Diana)
             Tray with 2 mugs of tea **(Diana)**
             Newspaper **(Chris)**
             Glass of white wine **(Diana)**
             2 mugs of coffee **(Diana)**
             Book **(Chris)**
             2 bags full of Christmas presents **(Chris)**

Personal: **Bob:** wrist-watch, lighted cigarette for beginning Act I
             Chris: wrist-watch, grannie glasses for reading
             Diana: large glasses for reading

ACT II

Strike: Bags full of Christmas presents
             Book
             Tablecloth

Set: Finished shelf unit L ⎫
             Another shelf unit C ⎬ with dressing on shelves
             Unfinished shelf unit US. *On it:* tin of varnish, brush. *Near it:* toolbag
             Shirt for **Diana**
             Child's shoe and duster for **Chris**
             Book, felt-tip pens, cardigan around room
             Child's shoe on sofa, other one on floor
             Iron, small screwdriver on table DL
             Packet of cigarettes, empty matchbox on coffee table
             Chisel and child's skate under cushion on sofa

Off stage: Light bulb in box **(Chris)**
             Book **(Diana)**
             Newspaper **(Chris)**
             Child's shirt, button, needle and thread **(Diana)**
             Dustpan and brush **(Chris)**
             Bowl of flowers **(Chris)**
             Car keys **(Diana)**
             Work book **(Diana)**

Personal: **Bob:** wrist-watch, rag in pocket, car keys, folded letter, handkerchief,
             another letter, lighter
             Chris: wrist-watch

LIGHTING PLOT

Practical fittings required: pendant light, 2 table lamps

Interior. 1 set representing 2 living-rooms. The same scene throughout

ACT I

To open: General evening lighting—practicals on

Cue 1	**Bob** (*nodding*): "Yeah." *Cross-fade to bright white lighting* DS	(Page 6)
Cue 2	**Bob** slumps into easy chair, putting down toolbag *Cross-fade to evening lighting—practicals on*	(Page 7)
Cue 3	**Diana** stands in doorway R; **Chris** enters L *Cross-fade to bright white lighting* DS	(Page 12)
Cue 4	**Bob:** ". . . eighteen months ago?" *Cross-fade to evening lighting—practicals on*	(Page 13)
Cue 5	**Chris:** "Then don't go." *Cross-fade to bright white lighting* DS	(Page 13)
Cue 6	**Bob:** "And . . . I met Diana." *Cross-fade to dim, warm, party lighting* DS	(Page 15)
Cue 7	**Bob:** "Why not?" **Diana** exits *Cross-fade to bright white lighting* DS	(Page 16)
Cue 8	**Bob:** "Big deal." *Cross-fade to general daytime lighting—no practicals*	(Page 16)
Cue 9	**Bob:** "Certainly." *Cross-fade to bright white lighting* DS	(Page 20)
Cue 10	**Bob:** ". . . that . . . is commitment." *Cross-fade to dim evening lighting—lamp* R *on*	(Page 21)
Cue 11	**Chris** goes out L *Pause, then cross-fade to bright white lighting* DS *and slightly* US	(Page 24)
Cue 12	**Diana** enters to stand in doorway R *Cross-fade to general daytime lighting*	(Page 25)
Cue 13	**Bob** puts shelf into place, banging it down *Cross-fade to bright white lighting* DS	(Page 28)
Cue 14	**Chris:** ". . . between Manor House and Cockfosters." *Dim lights to spot on chairs* DS	(Page 28)
Cue 15	**Chris:** "You coward." She gets up *Cross-fade to dim lighting*	(Page 28)

Cue 16	**Bob** switches on lamp L	(Page 29)
	Snap on lamp L	
Cue 17	**Bob** switches on pendant	(Page 29)
	Snap on pendant	
Cue 18	As sound of drill magnifies	(Page 32)
	Slowly dim lights to area round **Bob**	

ACT II

To open: Bright white lighting DS

Cue 19	**Bob** wipes his hands on rag	(Page 34)
	Cross-fade to evening lighting—practicals on	
Cue 20	**Diana** switches off pendant	(Page 37)
	Snap off pendant	
Cue 21	**Bob** tries main light	(Page 37)
	Snap on pendant	
Cue 22	**Bob** pulls out a folded letter	(Page 41)
	Cross-fade to bright white lighting DS	
Cue 23	**Bob** becomes dejected again, pocketing the letter	(Page 41)
	Cross-fade to warm evening lighting—practicals on	
Cue 24	**Bob** takes up cordless telephone and dials	(Page 43)
	Cross-fade to bright white lighting DS	
Cue 25	**Bob**, **Chris** and **Diana** sit on sofa	(Page 43)
	Cross-fade to lighting on sofa only	
Cue 26	**Bob:** "You've done enough already."	(Page 44)
	Cross-fade to evening lighting—practicals on	
Cue 27	**Chris** makes to exit, but stands in doorway, facing audience	(Page 47)
	Dim lights US, *bring up spot on* **Chris**	
Cue 28	**Chris** exits; **Diana** enters	(Page 47)
	Cross-fade to evening lighting—practicals on	
Cue 29	**Diana** goes out	(Page 49)
	Cross-fade to bright white lighting DS	
Cue 30	**Bob:** "... all she needed, I suppose."	(Page 50)
	Cross-fade to dim evening lighting—lamp R *on*	
Cue 31	**Chris** remains sitting, looking down at her clenched hands	(Page 52)
	Cross-fade to bright white lighting DS	
Cue 32	**Bob:** "I mean—commonsense."	(Page 52)
	Cross-fade to general lighting—no practicals	
Cue 33	**Chris** enters	(Page 55)
	Cross-fade to bright white lighting DS	
Cue 34	**Bob:** "... the cloud has a silver lifeboat."	(Page 57)
	Cross-fade to general daytime lighting	

Cue 35   **Chris:** "I really don't." She goes out   (Page 58)
          Cross-fade to dim evening lighting—lamp R *on*

Cue 36   **Diana** goes out, taking off her coat   (Page 59)
          Cross-fade to general daytime lighting—no practicals

Cue 37   **Bob:** ". . . flat in Parsons Green."   (Page 62)
          Begin to dim lights slowly

EFFECTS PLOT

ACT I

Cue 1   Before CURTAIN rises   (Page 1)
         3 knocks with a hammer, then sound of **Bob** *singing "Gonna Build
         A Mountain" and sawing—both becoming louder then suddenly
         stopping*

Cue 2   **Bob:** "And ... I met Diana."   (Page 15)
         Background noise of party and music

Cue 3   **Diana** exits R   (Page 16)
         Cut party noise and music

Cue 4   **Bob:** "... that ... is commitment."   (Page 21)
         Pause, then soft music from radio

Cue 5   **Bob** switches off radio   (Page 21)
         Cut music

Cue 6   **Chris:** "... between Manor House and Cockfosters."   (Page 28)
         Low sound of underground train

Cue 7   **Chris:** "You coward." She gets up   (Page 28)
         Cut train noise

Cue 8   **Chris** and **Diana** enter to stand in the doorways looking at him   (Page 32)
         *Sound of drill magnifies; then magnified sound of drilling and
         hammering, then magnified sound of drilling, hammering and
         sawing—continue until* CURTAIN *has fallen*

ACT II

Cue 9   Before CURTAIN rises   (Page 33)
         *Magnified sounds of drilling, hammering and sawing, then of
         drilling and hammering, then of drilling—cut as* CURTAIN *rises*

MADE AND PRINTED IN GREAT BRITAIN BY
LATIMER TREND & COMPANY LTD PLYMOUTH
MADE IN ENGLAND